I0569783

THE BOOK OF TAHL
From Homelessness to Paralympic Gold

Tahl Leibovitz

with

Sean O'Neill
Two-Time Olympian and Five-Time U.S. Champion

and

Jim Bergman

Foreword by Will Shortz

MediacsBooks
New Paltz, NY

MediacsBooks
36 Henry W. Dubois Drive, #8
New Paltz, New York 12561
www.mediacsbooks.com

Editor: Jim Bergman
Cover Design & Book Layout: Matthew Heister
Photo Fixing: Matthew Frederick

Ordering Information:
Quantity sales. Special discounts are available on quantity purchases by corporations, associations, and others. For details, contact the "Special Sales Department" at the address above.

The Book of Tahl/ Tahl Leibovitz
ISBN 978-8-9894765-9-6

Table of Contents

Foreword 1

About This Book 3

Birth 9

Childhood 13

South Queens Boys Club 33

Homeless 39

    Fighting 39

    Sleeping 48

    Eating 48

    Personal Hygiene 49

    Clothing 51

    Friendship 51

The Lost Battalion Club 59

Ill-Gainful Employment 63

Education 67

    Sean on Coaching Paralympic Athletes 85

Mentoring. 87

    Sean's Perspective On Our Partnership 88

My Anger Problem 93

Falling in Love - Slowly 97

    Doubling with Sean 99

    A Partner for Life 104

    The 2004 Summer Paralympics in Athens . . .106

    Mother's Deathbed Wish 108

    My Demons Return 114

    Angie and Stellan 121

U.S. Hall of Fame Induction 127

Social Work .129

The Present .139

Afterthoughts 141

For Serious Table Tennis Players 143

Match Results 147

Sean's Afterword 151

Competing against Hungary's Dezso Berecki, during a Paralympic
match in Rio on Sept. 10, 2016 (National Post)

Foreword

As the owner of a large table tennis club with major monthly tournaments, and as an avid player myself since childhood, I've met a lot of table tennis junkies.

Generally speaking, the sport attracts unusual people, myself included — some might call us "quirky." Partly this is because table tennis is an individual's sport. Winning or losing depends entirely on the person, not teammates. If you lose, there's no one to blame but yourself.

Partly it's because table tennis is brainy. It attracts people who like to use their intelligence and to strategize, both in training and in fast-moving matches.

And probably, in part, this is because table tennis isn't regarded as a major sport. It's not seen much on TV or covered much in the media. Although tens of millions of people play ping-pong casually, there are only a few hundred sanctioned table tennis clubs in the entire United States. To take the game seriously, you have to go out of your way.

Even among this unusual group of people, though, Tahl Leibovitz stands out. He's one of America's best players — for starters a Paralympic gold medalist, but a highly competitive player even among the able-bodied. Through sheer force of will as well as his natural abilities, he has overcome tremendous odds — and handicaps — to achieve his success.

Tahl has a fascinating life story, told here in his own words.

-Will Shortz
Owner, Westchester Table Tennis Center
Crossword Editor, The New York Times

About This Book

This memoir has been many difficult years in the making. Previous efforts to write about my childhood and teenage homelessness churned up deeply entrenched traumas that made the process exceptionally difficult and unsettling. Except for brief passages, I was seriously writer blocked.

It was not until I collaborated with Jim Bergman, my editor and table tennis student, that the process began to flow. Instead of sitting at my desk, alone with my thoughts, writing down my life story, Jim conducted several hours of taped interviews in person or on Zoom, which together we transcribed into this work of memoir.

I think this approach worked well because it matched my philosophy of helping others as a social worker and psychotherapist. The success of my work, as I see it, flows from a genuine and healthy collaboration between me and the people I try to help. Just like this memoir flowed from a collaboration between me and Jim.

Why did I want to write my memoir? For many reasons.

I'm in the business of helping people overcome their difficulties in life, everything from intrusive thoughts, anxiety and depression, and bipolar disorder to schizophrenia and substance abuse. Maybe my memoir will reach more people who need help. Give them hope that they, too, can overcome the adversities that I faced.

I was also motivated by the fact that many people do not see the person behind the professional athlete. Not so long ago, I had a conversation with a female boxer who won a bronze medal at the Olympics. She told me she was homeless the entire time she was competing. Her story is worth telling, too.

Another reason why I wrote my memoir was to demonstrate how a passion for a sport can provide safe shelter for somebody whose life was cut adrift by parental abuse and homelessness. Without my love for table tennis, my overarching desire to get really good at it, I might be dead or spending my life behind bars.

Finally, I felt my memoir would serve as a heartfelt thank you to all the people in my life who mentored me throughout my many years of personal struggle.

I've changed the names of my street friends. Most of them, like myself, have gone on to live normal, respectful lives far removed from the violence and criminality of our previous life on the streets.

4

At the end of this memoir, I've written a short section for table tennis fans and players called For Serious Table Tennis Players. Some of this material also appears in *Ping Pong for Fighters; Gold Medal Edition*, a book I wrote and published in 2017.

Ping Pong for Fighters; Gold Medal Edition

I've asked my coach and mentor, Sean O'Neill, the man who's had a profoundly positive impact on my development as a person, athlete, social worker and therapist, to add his comments both to the body of this memoir (in italics), and to the back of this book in an Afterword. Readers who wish to delve deeper into the mentoring and coaching of a man I consider a father-figure, and to the strategy and tactics of my most memorable matches, will enjoy reading Sean's contributions.

Sean and me in a recent photo

This is my story. A story of how my determination to become a top professional table tennis competitor helped me overcome the stigma of being physically disabled and survive the obstacles of homelessness and petty crime. It is also a story that involved many others who mentored me along the way such as my coach, Sean O'Neill, who helped me immensely as a professional table tennis player, get through school, become a licensed social worker and psychotherapist, and forge a healthy balance between the demands of professional sport and life outside the tournament hall.

I'm 49-years-old and still going strong. Last year (2023), I competed in over a dozen able-bodied and Paralympic tournaments held throughout the world. Right now, I'm training for the U.S. Nationals in July and the 2024 Summer Paralympics in Paris. And although I'm still winning most of my matches and finishing in the top three medal categories of many tournaments, I have to work harder than ever before to remain competitive.

Proper diet and weight management, daily table tennis practice, and several miles of walking (my favorite exercise) each day are just as crucial to an older athlete's success as his or her competitive spirit.

Birth

I was born in Haifa, Israel, in 1975, 20 minutes after my twin sister, Maja, whose delivery was normal. Mine was a breech birth. My feet were twisted and deformed. Non-cancerous bone tumors proliferated throughout my body, and my feet and hands sweated excessively: two afflictions, osteochondroma and hyperhidrosis, inherited from my mother's side of the family.

My mother never forgave me for my painful birth. Only the devil, she said, would cause her such pain. The voices in her head told her so.

Both my parents' families were deeply traumatized by wartime experiences. My maternal grandfather, Simon Weisskohl, was an Auschwitz survivor who was rescued by the Swedish White Cross. Every member of his Polish family, including his parents and seven siblings, were murdered by the Nazis, most of them before his very eyes. After the war, he settled down in Sweden, married and had a child, my mother, Felicia.

My father's family lived in Bucharest. Shortly before the start of the Second World War, they sent their five-year-old daughter, Gitl, to live with an aunt in Transylvania. Gitl had pneumonia, and her parents hoped the cool mountain air would help heal her lungs. In August 1940, when the Third Reich annexed Northern Transylvania, Gitl and her aunt's family were rounded up by the Nazis and sent to Auschwitz where they were murdered. Ernest's family survived the Nazi occupation of Hungary because his father, a skilled cabinet maker and carpenter, was protected by a client of German descent who worked for the new government.

9

My Aunt Gitl who perished in Auschwitz

My father, Ernest Leibovitz, was born in 1947, two years after the end of the Second World War. In 1961, he and his family emigrated to Israel.

My father fought with the Israeli Tank Corps in both the Six Day War of 1967 and the Yom Kippur War of October 1973. In the latter conflict, the Israeli Tank Corps was destroyed by a Syrian ambush on the Golan Heights in a nighttime battle. Unlike the Syrian tanks, the Israeli tanks were not equipped with night vision, and all 11 of them were destroyed. My dad managed to get out of his tank after it was hit. A few minutes later, it was hit by a second shell and exploded. Fortunately, three Israeli tanks came up behind the Syrian tanks and forced them to flee. My father jumped on one of the tanks and rode it back to friendly territory.

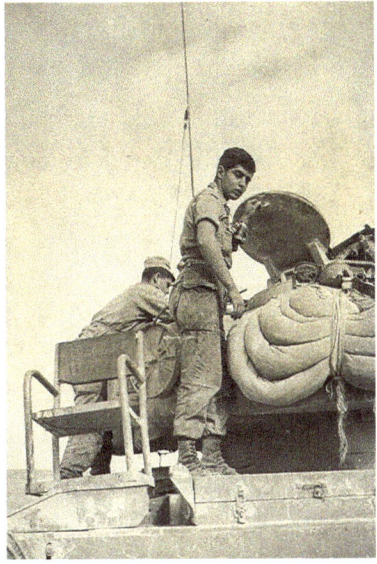

My father, Ernest Leibovitz,
Israeli Tank Commander

The next day, while showering, he noticed the right side of his body was plastered with small bits of shrapnel. He still has some of them in his body.

A few years after the war ended, my mother's family also emigrated to Israel and then to the U.S. where they settled in Rockaway Beach, New York. My grandfather Simon owned and ran a sweater factory in the Brooklyn.

When she was a teenager, my mother and her brother spent summers working in their father's factory in Brooklyn. When she tried to unionize the illegal immigrants who worked long hours for very little pay in her father's factory, Simon was infuriat-ed. When she dated a Black American man, his

11

sense of Jewish piousness was deeply offended. So he sent her to Haifa, Israel in 1971, to go to school.

In Israel, my mother failed the University of Haifa's entrance exam because she did not speak or write Hebrew. She met my father, Ernest, at a disco in Haifa, the 120 Club, where they both were employed. They married on December 30, 1971, under pressure from Felicia's father.

After Felicia got pregnant with my older sister, Cecilia, my father abandoned his rock 'n' roll band and DJ career, and earned a certificate in computer programing from ORT, a vocational college.

Both my parents were well-read and highly educated. My mother went to Queens College and earned master's degrees in Education and Anthropology. My father spoke several languages and was an avid reader since the age of five.

My mother was also a borderline psychotic who heard voices. My father was a perfectionist, grandiose narcissist and alcoholic. Both were incredibly negligent and abusive parents.

Childhood

In 1975, seven months after Maja and I were born, our family emigrated from Haifa to Flatbush, Brooklyn. We moved again in 1981 to Howard Beach, an Italian American neighborhood in the southwestern part of the New York City borough of Queens. We lived in a modest two-bedroom co-op in a four-family building, a gift from my mother's father, Simon, who paid $8,000 for the co-op. All three of us kids shared one of two bedrooms. Our older sister Cecilia slept in a bed. Maja and I slept in a bunk bed.

Maja and me were four when this photo
was taken with our older sister, Cecilia.

The neighborhood was economically divided by the Belt Parkway. We lived on the Lindenwood side, a community of condos, coops and apartment buildings inhabited by working and lower middle-class families. The rich folks lived in houses on the other side of the parkway. It wasn't a depressing neighborhood, but there were a lot of restrictions imposed by the co-op boards. As soon as you entered the coop community you were greeted by a big sign which said, "No Ball Playing, No Running." A list of rules which were difficult to miss.

Me and Maja, age 6, at home in Howard Beach.

There was a large supermarket in a nearby shopping center where we hung out, and a swampland about a mile from our home where we built a clubhouse.

Homelife was difficult. Our father was drunk most days. He had a good job working for a data processing firm, but he kept showing up for work inebriated and was eventually fired. For the next two or three years, he was unemployed. Eventually, he found a job with a New York City agency he was able to hold.

My father also had a gambling problem. He often went to Atlantic City and lost what little money he had, and he played the gambling machines at the bars he patronized in the evenings.

It is possible the trauma of my father's experience in the Yom Kippur War, watching his platoon members being killed, may be the source of his alcohol and gambling problems. He may suffer from Post-Traumatic Stress Disorder (PTSD).

My mother, tired of not having money, decided to go back to school and become a schoolteacher. She enrolled at Queens College, CUNY, and completed two master's degrees. She taught in Brownsville, Brooklyn elementary and junior high schools.

The day my sister Cecilia graduated from junior high school. Maja and I were ten years old.

When my parents weren't screaming at each other, usually about money, they were angry at Maja and me.

Dad was usually nicer to us kids when he was intoxicated. If we wanted to buy something, we always waited until he was very drunk to ask him for money. When he was sober, he

16

was an out-of-control drill sergeant, abusive and controlling. He complained often about having to spend money on us kids who he said wouldn't amount to much in life. Having to buy us bus passes was one of his frequent gripes.

Although our mother had steady teaching jobs, our family was always short of money. We wore second-hand clothes bought at rummage and yard sales. We ate cheap and unnourishing meals: empty taco shells, a box of rice pilaf, or a homemade spinach pie that made us vomit. Occasionally, we were on public assistance. Without the financial support of my mother's father, my grandfather Simon, we would have been homeless.

My mother was very health conscious. A big fan of Gary Null, radio's popular health guru at the time, she forbade salt, sugar and processed food. She also walked a lot, practiced yoga and wrote poetry. She was 5'2" tall and in good physical shape.

My mother spoke Swedish, the language of her birth country. My father was fluent in most Slavic and European languages. At home, they spoke Hebrew and English. When Maja and I were three, and Maja still did not speak at all, my mother consulted a language specialist. "You must speak only English at home," the specialist advised. Maja started speaking English soon afterwards, and I lost my Hebrew-English bilingualism.

Reading books and writing book reports was a mainstay of my childhood — a welcome relief from the constant physical abuse by my father and the delusional rantings of my mother. Every week, we had to choose a book from our parents' overflowing bookshelves and write a report, for which we were paid $1.00. My favorite books were science fiction classics written by

Robert Heinlen and Phillip K. Dick, and mysteries by Richard Safer and Warren Murphy.

Maja and me in front of the family's bookcases.
"It's important to read," our parents told us.

Doing our school homework was a terrible ordeal. It provoked our father's worst character traits, his drill sergeant mentality and need to be smarter and better than anyone else. He made us sit for hours in the living room writing and rewriting book reports for school on lined pads until they were in his opinion absolutely perfect in both content and appearance. Perfection was something he cared deeply about and seldom achieved in his own life.

"You'll never amount to anything," he told us. He wanted us to be just like him.

He was also physically abusive. If we walked ahead of him on the sidewalk, he'd yell: "Don't walk in front of me" and kick the backs of our legs. At home, when we did or said something he didn't like, he'd slap us with his hands or a metal ruler. Maja would curl up on the floor in a fetal position and take the blows on her legs. I'd try to outrun him. He often beat me with his belt.

When I was five, my mother arranged for me to have a therapy session. The therapist asked me to draw a picture of my family. I drew a picture of my father with a huge X through his body. A year later, worried about my intellectual development, my mother arranged for me to take an I.Q. test. She told me my score was 149.

* * *

A child who is abused by his parents identifies with his abuser or with the victim (himself). I identified with myself, the helpless, out-of-control victim, and behaved as I felt. That might help explain my hyperactive behavior in school.

* * *

When I was nine, my father complained about having to give us children money for bus passes. That was when I realized he didn't really care about us kids, that he cared only for himself. From that day until now, I have tried my best to block him out of my life as much as possible.

Maja remembers the day he overheard me tell her, "Dad's an asshole," and quick-marched me into his bedroom for a proper belting. I always stood up to him, verbally. Physically, there was

19

not much I could do. I often imagined about how I would hurt him when I became a grown man.

* * *

Many years later, my father told a reporter writing a profile of me that his harsh discipline was just his way of making me tough and strong. "I wasn't hitting him because I was getting mad and upset. I was hitting him because I was trying to make a point," he said. "My son was a problematic teenager."

I know now, as a trained and practicing psychotherapist, how much psychological damage physical abuse inflicts on children.

* * *

My defiance, Maja says, got me into a lot of trouble, not only with our dad, but also with my classmates who were much bigger than me and didn't like Jewish people. One kid in particular always wanted to fight me. Sometimes he brought another kid with him to fight me, too. They'd come to my house, after school and on the weekends, and call me out.

My early school years were spent trying to avoid these bullies. Although we lived diagonally across the street from school, I walked a different roundabout route home every day. When my father asked me why it took me up to an hour to get home after school, I told him: "I have enemies."

When they did catch me, they never really hurt me much, unlike my father. They pushed me around. I pushed them back. They knocked the books out of my hands. Called me a kike and other bad names. I cursed them out, too. Always stood up to them, though they were bigger and could beat me up.

In retrospect, I now realize I did feel shame about being Jewish. I was just a kid, hoping to fit in, be accepted. I was too young to know it's okay to be Jewish. Or whatever other religion you want to be.

But what really disturbed these bullies was they couldn't intimidate me. I met them on their level. If they were not riled up, I would stay calm. If they yelled at me, I yelled back. I never let them think I was scared of them. Even when they pushed me around.

I always tried to stand up to my father, too, though I was definitely much more scared of him because he did beat me badly, really inflicted pain. I never showed him how badly he hurt me. Wouldn't give him that satisfaction.

* * *

Maja's right. I've always been defiant. Not sure where it came from. Maybe from my grandfather, Simon, who escaped from two Nazi extermination camps and survived Auschwitz. Simon also spoke his mind. Whatever its source, my defiance shielded me from my father's physical and mental abuse. Helped me not let it get under my skin.

My father was also defiant. He was constantly complaining about authority, about rules. But I don't think he played a part in shaping my defiant nature because what he often said was so painful, I just tuned him out from the age of nine or ten.

Our mother was also abusive, emotionally and physically. If we said or did something that made her angry, she'd pick up a kitchen knife or broomstick and chase us around the apartment. She never really tried to cut us with the knife, but she did hit us with the broomstick.

Most of the time, she was very distant from me and Maja. She wasn't physically affectionate or loving. And she never ever stopped reminding me I was the devil who caused her such pain in childbirth. But despite all that, deep down inside me, I knew she really cared for me. Unlike my father.

When I was 11, she took me on a visit to Sweden, her birth country, along with Hadar, the child fathered by her Trinidadian boyfriend — one of her many extramarital lovers.

Her relationship with Maja was much more troubled. She dressed Maja in tattered clothing and called her schmatta, the Yiddish word for rags. She told Maja she was too "ugly" to be taken outside. She gave her a short boy's haircut, just like her own haircut, and told her she was embarrassed that Maja was her daughter.

Our mother could also be very cruel. Although she forbade us to eat sugar or junk food, she often sat at the kitchen table eating an eggplant parmesan hero from the local pizza shop while we stood nearby, begging for a bite, which she never gave us.

Most days, she would rage against our father. If an argument broke out near dinner time, which was fairly often, Maja and I would go to bed hungry. That is one of my very worse childhood memories.

My mother heard voices that told her to walk down certain streets. She complained men were watching and following her. She told us she was a Black boy in another life. Or an anthropologist. She would lock herself in her bedroom and talk to herself for hours on end. She was in great mental pain.

* * *

I know now, having been trained as a psychotherapist, that my mother was bipolar and delusional, disorders possibly rooted in the abusive physical behavior of her father. She often complained to us about how my grandfather slammed doors on her fingers to punish her when she was a child. True or false, this is what she remembered. What she felt.

* * *

My father was a narcissistic, abusive alcoholic. My mother was mentally unstable. How could I take either of them seriously? My defiant nature stepped up to the plate, prevented me from blaming myself for their abusive behavior or internalizing their negative opinion of me.

Maja had a harder time blocking out our parents' negative treatment, not internalizing it. She's much stronger now, but it's definitely been more difficult for her to overcome the demeaning behavior of our parents.

Our older sister, Cecilia, was spared. Cecilia had an emotional breakdown soon after we settled in Howard Beach, and our parents treated her much nicer than they treated me and Maja. That explains why Cecilia's childhood memories are much different than ours. It's as if she grew up in another home with different parents.

When I was very young, my mother tried to straighten my twisted feet by binding them with Band-Aids — which didn't work. Finally, when I was ten, she took me to a podiatrist in Manhattan. I remember that journey, walking a mile-and-a-half to the A train because we lived in a two-fare zone from Manhattan and didn't want to pay for extra fares.

The podiatrist fitted me for orthotics, which I naturally outgrew in a few weeks. But my mother didn't take me back for a refitting for three years. The doctor was very upset. If I had continued wearing orthotics, he told her, my feet would be much improved. Now it was too late. I think my mother felt very bad about her negligence, though she didn't show me any regret.

Like me, my mother and her father also suffer from hyperhidrosis, excessive sweating of the feet and hands — a very rare affliction affecting one in five million people. There are three different degrees of this illness. I have the highest degree. My mother had surgery to correct this condition, an operation on the nerve in her neck that doctors believe causes or contributes to the ailment. The operation was not successful. It left one of her eyes bigger than the other, and didn't stop the excessive sweating.

* * *

When I compete in a major tournament, I need at least 49 pairs of socks to get through the three-to-five days of competition. Often, I'll need to put on a dry pair of socks in the middle of a match. I once tried playing a whole day without changing socks, but when I got home that night, my feet were drenched and I had painful blisters on the soles of my feet. Excessive sweating is definitely a nuisance. But I've never let it impact my performance.

* * *

My mother and father had an open marriage. My mother had many boyfriends, mostly African American men, some of whom she brought into our apartment when my father was not home. That didn't bother our father who also had girlfriends. If she was having a problem with one of her boyfriends, she turned to her husband for help and advice. And when she had a child by one of her extramarital lovers — my youngest sister, Hadar — our father put his name on Hadar's birth certificate and raised her as if she was his own child. He was incredibly supportive and loving of anything our mother did, perhaps because he understood how damaged she was by her own abusive childhood.

When I was six, I started having trouble falling asleep. I would lay awake in bed for hours, no matter how tired I was, reading comic books. Getting up in the morning in time for school was extremely difficult and often impossible.

* * *

My insomnia went untreated until 2003 when I was 28 years old. My U.S. Paralympic coach at the time, Stellan Bengtsson, the great Swedish table tennis champion, arranged for me to be examined by a student of his who happened to be one of the country's leading sleep specialists. The specialist told me I was suffering from Delayed Phase Sleep Syndrome, a heightened sensitivity to light. He prescribed a regimen of melatonin at night and the use of a lightbox in the morning.

Delayed Phase Sleep Syndrome is associated with Attention Deficit/Hyperactivity Disorder (ADHD), which in turn often produces ADHD Hyperfocus — an intense fixation on an activity for an extended period of time.

I believe this offshoot of ADHD has helped me become a successful professional table tennis athlete. When I play at a tournament in front of thousands of people, I don't see or hear anything other than my opponent's ball hitting his racquet. Sean O'Neill, my longtime coach and mentor, is convinced that my extraordinarily high level of concentration is a key factor in my success as a professional table tennis professional.

That makes a lot of sense. Table tennis is a game of 11 points. If a professional player loses focus for a moment and drops a few points, it's likely he or she will lose that game.

My ADHD Hyperfocus was more likely a defense mechanism developed when I was a child. What my parents said to me was so painful, I became very good at blocking their comments and tuning them out.

Insomnia is no longer a constant problem for me, though if I'm not totally exhausted when I go to bed, falling asleep is still difficult.

* * *

When I was eight or nine, I had conversations with imaginary people who were dressed in drab grey clothing and were very mysterious. Internal dialogue with ourselves, especially when we are very young, is not unusual. But my imagined conversations were with people I didn't know or recognize. Which is unusual.

My problem with imaginary characters would resurface six years later in a much more dangerous and disturbing manner when I was homeless and living on the subway.

The trauma of living with abusive parents produces many aberrant behaviors and problems. My insomnia and internal dialogue with imaginary people stem in large part from the harsh and irrational behavior of my parents, as well as the heightened stress of living on the streets of New York City.

* * *

Maja and I were ten years old when our parents gathered us in the living room and told us they were separating and we'd be living with our mother in Woodhaven, Queens. They were worried the news would upset us and tried to soften the blow. We pretended to be shocked and unhappy, but were really thrilled by the unexpected news. No longer would we have to live with our abusive alcoholic father.

Our mother sold the co-op in Howard Beach for $90,000, and together they bought a house in Woodhaven for $149,000. Maintaining the house was always difficult for them, financially.

The two most disturbing facts of my childhood were going to bed hungry, and the abusive behavior of my father. When I was very young, as I mentioned earlier, I would daydream about becoming a man and inflicting physical pain on him.

27

Woodhaven was once called Woodville because it has one of the largest tree populations in Queens. When my family moved into the neighborhood in 1986, it was also home to a lot of fighting. The high school I went to, Franklin K. Lane High School, was eventually closed down because of the constant and often violent fighting among the students.

Shortly after my 12th birthday, I was walking down Jamaica Avenue, the neighborhood's main thoroughfare, with some bags of potato chips when a much older and bigger kid ran up to me, punched me in the face four or five times, stomped on my bags of potato chips, spit on me and calmly walked into a pizza parlor down the block as if nothing unusual had just occurred. Somehow, I managed not to fall down on the ground during this unprovoked assault.

I decided to go back home, a short journey of a block and a half. With each step, my feeling of being wrongly victimized became more intense. I knew I had to do something about it. Nothing else in the world mattered. I had to get that guy. He had to pay for attacking me.

My mother was sitting in the living room when I got home, watching her favorite soap opera, "Loving." My father used to say her life was a soap opera because that's all she watched.

I went to my bedroom, grabbed my backpack, went to the kitchen, and put a butcher's knife in my backpack. The same knife my mother held in the air while chasing me and Maja around the house, screaming "the blood is going to pour."

* * *

Our mother never cut us, though she came close a few times. After a while, her knife threats didn't scare me, seemed almost normal. But her out-of-control raging always felt strange and deeply disturbing.

* * *

I walked back to the pizza parlor. There he was, sitting in a booth with a friend. I took the knife out of my backpack, and moved quickly toward my assailant. Strangely, I no longer felt anger. I just felt intensely focused on what I had to do — cut his face open. I pulled the knife back. He saw me. Fear engulfed his face. He wasn't so strong anymore. He was a weak human being.

I stood there, knife drawn, staring at his face, long enough for one of the pizza parlor's workers to grab me from behind and disarm me. I ran out of the parlor and went home.

With all that focused intent and determination, you would think I'd be strong enough to prevent anyone from stopping me. But I wasn't strong enough. I hesitated.

Why did I hesitate? I think it was because the fear I saw in his eyes was the same fear I felt when my father was about to attack me. Stabbing him would be stabbing myself. That fear was our shared humanity.

What did I learn from this experience? Feeling wronged and treated unjustly can muster tremendous intent and physical energy. It's like an addiction. Hard to stop, no matter how damaging it is to yourself and other people. When I entered the pizza parlor wielding a butcher's knife, I was controlled by an overwhelming need to inflict pain on my attacker, a feeling I couldn't resist or control.

That was the last time in my life I hesitated to inflict pain on somebody who physically attacked me without provocation. When somebody attacks you, unprovoked, with or without a weapon, they are violent. If you don't defend yourself, you may spend the rest of your life regretting it. The world is a violent place, so it's better to be a warrior in a garden than a gardener in a war. You have to be able to stand up for yourself. That's why I think everyone should do some martial arts training so that they can defend themselves if someone attacks them.

* * *

In table tennis, I try not to see the shared humanity of my opponents until the match is completed. At the 2020 Paralympics in Tokyo, that actually took place in 2021, I was doing very well, winning my way into the medal round, until I happened to watch a short documentary about my upcoming opponent, a Ukrainian player, in the Class 9 Singles quarterfinals. The documentary described his impoverished background and how he overcame terrible adversaries. When I was up 6-2 in the fifth and deciding game of our quarterfinal, I suddenly felt bad about beating him — feelings which distracted me and lost me the match.

* * *

A few years earlier, I was in Manhattan walking past a clothing store where some teenagers were stealing items. When the manager confronted them, one of the teenagers cut his face with a razor blade. It happened so fast the manager didn't realize he'd been cut until he started bleeding from the corner of his right eye. There was blood everywhere.

Human beings are fragile. We can be hurt easily. And we can hurt others easily.

South Queens Boys Club

South Queens Boys and Girls Club in 2023

My father remembers being called to school on several occasions and being told by my teachers that they simply couldn't get me to sit still in class. I don't recall hyperactivity being a problem in grade school. I do recall my mother coming to school and complaining that my 3rd grade teacher was being very abusive. She demanded the teacher be fired. The teacher was not fired, but she did treat me much nicer after my mother's visit.

A few weeks into the 8th grade, I became a truant. Unable to fall asleep at a reasonable hour, I just couldn't get up early enough to go to school on time, and I was tired of avoiding the bullies who wanted to fight me because I was Jewish and much smaller than they were. So most school days I stayed at home listening to music when Mom was at work, or packed up my schoolbooks and hung out on the street with other disaffected truants. My mother knew I was often truant, and that someone, probably a teacher, had filed a Persons in Need of Supervision (PINS) petition in family court.

In 1989, when I was 14, she enrolled me in the afterschool program of the South Queens Boys Club on Atlantic Avenue. She wanted me to have somewhere safe to hang out after school.

I remember my first day at the club, walking into that old broken-down building with my mother for a meeting with the club's director, Leo Compton.

Leo knew I was skipping school. "You can be a member of this club as long as you go to school," he told me. "If I find out you're not going to school, you will not be welcome here. Got it?"

Leo didn't mince words. He was a matter-of-fact tough guy who talked with a heavy Brooklyn accent, swore a lot, and dressed like a biker in leather jackets. Over the years, Leo and I had many loud heated disagreements, mostly about my not showing up at school.

After the interview ended and my mother went home, I walked into the club's large recreational room where kids were shooting pool and playing table tennis on two old, dimly lit battered sawhorse tables. I felt that heavy feeling you get entering a potentially dangerous environment. The kids were tough, delinquent and physically aggressive. About a year later, one of them murdered a taxicab driver and was sent to prison for life. Most towered over my 5'3" frame and easily outweighed my 110 lbs. I didn't get into a fight that first day at the club, but I certainly had my share of them in coming months. Not because I was Jewish. Because fighting was just something we did.

Back then, the kids at the Boys Club played with sandpaper or hard rubber paddles — not the smooth-surfaced sponge rubber paddles used today. The club didn't have the resources to buy new racquets, tables or nets.

* * *

Today, table tennis is played on three different surfaces. Sandpaper, hard-bat (a hard, ribbed rubber surface) and sponge with a smooth rubber surface. Sponge is by far the most popular used by a majority of professional players, but there are separate tournaments for all three.

* * *

While I also played handball at the club, I soon settled on table tennis as my sport of choice. When I was nine or ten, I competed in a neighborhood summer tournament for children and adults, and won first place despite never having played table tennis. So I just assumed that table tennis was a sport I could get really good at.

I was easily the very worst player at the club. Holding a paddle in my excessively sweaty hand was difficult, especially in the summer. Moving laterally on my deformed feet was also difficult. And not being able to extend my shorter right arm or flex my right wrist — thanks to the benign bone tumors scattered throughout my body — seriously handicapped my game.

Some of the kids refused to play with me. Others chided me for even trying to play. "Go find yourself another sport," they told me. "You'll never get good at ping pong."

That just made me even more determined to become better than them. Beat them! Show them I was just as physically capable as they were. Although none of these kids ever called me disabled, or a cripple, that's what I heard them say. I didn't think of myself as a disabled person, and I wasn't going to allow anyone else to think of me in that way, either.

The shame of being a person with physical disabilities, which I definitely was, obviously ran deep inside me — even though I was totally unaware of it at the time.

Over the next few months, I adapted my physical disabilities to the sport. To overcome the disadvantage of a fixed right wrist, I changed my grip on the handle so that I could hit the ball with the proper racquet angle. To compensate for not being able to move fast laterally, I switched racquet hands in the middle of a point so I could return angled crosscourt shots without having to move quickly to the other side of the table.

It took me six months to develop a reliable backhand, and another six months to become truly competitive and start winning the majority of games against other members of the boy's club.

* * *

Table tennis is the most disabled-friendly sport. It's not unusual to see an 85-year-old man with limited mobility play a nine-year-old girl at a major table tennis tournament. Or a person in a wheelchair playing someone with an amputated limb, arm or leg, who's holding a walking stick in one hand and a table tennis racquet in the other.

* * *

About a year after I began playing table tennis at the South Queens Boys Club, the players transitioned to smooth rubber paddles which produce far more spin and speed than sandpaper paddles. Once again I had to adapt the game to my physical disabilities. By varying the placement and spin of the ball — topspin, sidespin, underspin and no spin — I was able to compensate for my inability to move quickly by disrupting my opponents' rhythm. Very few players are able to move me around the table.

Homeless

Shortly after my 14th birthday, I broke the basement window of my mother's house with a soccer ball I was kicking around in the backyard. When I got home for dinner that night, Maja told me: "Mom and Dad are very upset you broke the window. Dad was here earlier. He said he's going to come back and kill you."

When my father said that, which he did quite often, a bad beating invariably followed. Not this time, I decided. This time I was going to get away from him for good. So I threw some things into my backpack — shirts, socks, a toothbrush and my table tennis racquet, which went with me wherever I went — and high-tailed it onto the streets.

I would spend most of the next few years sleeping in subway cars or on rooftops, stealing food from restaurants and supermarkets, shop-lifting clothing and electronic devices from deparment stores and shops, and endlessly fighting off the hordes of people, mostly older kids, who prey on homeless people.

Fighting

That first night on the streets, the J train was my bedroom of choice. I boarded the first car and had a peaceful journey to the end of the line. But when the car turned around for its return trip, I was in the last car, just where you don't want to be, isolated and alone. Sure enough, three older kids of about 18 or 19 got into the car and asked me if I had any money. "I don't have any money," I told them. "I'm homeless." For some reason, that really annoyed them. "Okay," their ringleader said, "we'll take your backpack instead."

I had never been comfortable with physical altercations. Avoided them when I could, and never really fought back. When my father attacked me with a metal ruler or belt, I couldn't fight back because he was so much bigger and stronger. And on those rare occasions when the school bullies caught me, I knew they weren't really out to hurt me badly. So fighting back would have been super dumb, just made them more angry and violent.

But now, cornered in a subway car by three older kids intent on stealing all my worldly possessions, I had no option but to fight back. So when they threw punches at me, for the first time in my life, I hit back. I even tried to bite one of the kid's face. I did everything I could to survive. After a minute of flailing about, we were all gasping for breath, totally out of air. When the train got to the next station, they just calmly walked out of the car without my backpack. Fortunately, for me, they weren't armed.

When you live on the streets and subways, it's impossible to avoid fighting. Most confrontations do not involve weapons and last for about 20-to-30 seconds before everybody runs out of energy and just stops fighting. When an unarmed person tried to steal my backpack, I knew it was unlikely I'd be seriously hurt.

Even when somebody with a weapon attacked me, I never got seriously hurt. I'm not strong, and I'm disabled. But sometimes my shortness and disability were definite advantages. That's because most of the people who tried to rob me on the street and subway were over-confident when they confronted me. A short little guy like me couldn't hurt them, they figured. So when I did hurt them, they were confused and quickly broke off their attack.

* * *

I have the same advantage playing table tennis when able-bodied opponents assume a short little disabled guy like me doesn't stand a chance of beating them. If I move back from the table and counterattack forehand to forehand, like most really skilled players, I'll lose at least 80 percent of the points because my opponents simply have more range of motion and are stronger. But if I vary the height, depth and pace of the ball, and play closer to the table, I can disrupt their normal way of playing the game and force them to adapt, which most opponents are unable to do.

* * *

When people tried to rob me at gun or knife point, that raised the confrontation into the realm of violence. I woke up on the subway one night with a knife to my stomach. Occasionally, I was held up at gun point. Three kids assaulted me with razor blades, but luckily I was wearing a large, padded jacket which got sliced up instead of me. All of them wanted my money or backpack. None of them succeeded.

In a fight, you battle with someone for a few minutes, and then it's over. Either your attacker hurts you more, or you hurt him more. But when weapons are involved, you are in a violent confrontation and in danger of being seriously maimed or even killed.

After a while, I got good at figuring out the mentality of an attacker. If they had mental issues or were on drugs —

41

something you can usually tell from their appearance — they will want to hurt you, even kill you. Others will fight you, but don't have a killer mentality, or are more afraid of being hurt themselves. Knowing who to fight and who to avoid fighting is a key to survival on the street.

* * *

In a table tennis match, knowing how and when an opponent will attack you is what coaches call "anticipation" — a subconscious process of gathering information about the mindset of the other player and adapting to the competition. It's the same on the street. In a table tennis match, you can sometimes use your opponent's energy against him or her. In a street fight, you can also use your attacker's energy against him.

* * *

When someone attacked me, I tried to harm them first. They were invariably much bigger and stronger, and, unlike me, able-bodied. I punched them in the throat, bit them, did anything to disarm them and allow me to get away. If I didn't harm them, they would harm me. And if I succeeded in inflicting pain on them, they would normally retreat.

The only time I would attack someone was when it was obvious they meant to harm me. When someone told me they just wanted to check my pockets for money, I knew from experience that when they came up empty handed, they would get angry and attack me. So while they were rummaging through my pockets, I'd attack them first when they weren't expecting it.

Occasionally, I was confronted on the street by individuals who I realized would not be deterred by any amount of pain I might inflict upon them. Knowing they would fight me to the end, the only recourse was to somehow placate them or get away. Fortunately, these extremely dangerous people were in the minority.

My table tennis training helped me become a better fighter. It made me very proficient in transferring body weight into the ball from both my backhand and forehand sides. If I held a hard object in either hand, I could strike a blow with every ounce of my 110 lbs. behind it, even though my arm traveled a very short distance. Like Bruce Lee's one-inch punch, my blow often stopped an attacker almost immediately.

Martial arts and table tennis are remarkably similar. Whatever school of martial arts you practice, arm and leg movements are short in distance and immensely powerful. The same is true with table tennis. In both sports, basic angles and body weight transfer are vital so that force is applied with little movement. The table tennis paddle is actually a force magnifier.

* * *

I've always been interested in martial arts. Today I practice a mix of martial arts. After the 2024 Summer Paralympics in Paris, I will start martial arts training five days a week. It's very enjoyable and in each training session you can burn on average 490-800 calories.

After my life of living on the streets ended, I've only had to use my martial arts skills twice. Once when I was attacked at a party by two people, and another time when I stopped a guy beating a woman with a motorcycle chain. I was with a friend, a social worker like me, driving along Queens Boulevard when we saw a big muscle guy with a pit bull beating up a girl with a motorcycle chain. Luckily, my friend and I were able to fight off both the pit bull and the guy. My friend was carrying a baseball bat, which was super helpful.

Nowadays, mostly everyone trains in some kind of martial art. But it's always best to avoid fights when you can and only get into an altercation if you have absolutely no other choice.

* * *

After a few months of homelessness, I stopped worrying about getting into fights. I was invincible. Nothing could hurt me. I'd get into a fight without worrying what would happen to me. Like soldiers who go into battle, not knowing if they'll live or die, I accepted the possibility I would be hurt or even killed. So when someone pointed a gun or knife at me, and said "give me your backpack," I said, "there's nothing of value in here, and I'm not going to let you take it, anyway."

This God-like feeling of invincibility lasted many years. It was intoxicating. I still miss it today. But what I don't miss is the downside of that intoxicating feeling, not caring about living or dying, the self-doubt about the value of my life. If I didn't care about living or dying, why live?

Suicidal ideation became part of my daily thoughts. Suicide would not only end a life that I did not value, but it would have the added benefit of erasing the painful memories of my childhood that just wouldn't go away. So shortly after becoming homeless at

14, I started cutting my wrists, not across veins but lengthwise. Obviously, my intention to kill myself was experimental and half-hearted. A more serious attempt would come 15 years later in 2009 when I was married and a world-famous Paralympic athlete.

* * *

Jim asked me to imagine sitting in my office providing psycho-therapy to myself as a homeless teenager. What would be my diagnosis and recommended treatment? That was easy. My diagnosis would be Persistent Depression Disorder or what psychothera-pists call a common symptomyology of depression and anxiety, along with Post Traumatic Stress Disorder (PTSD) and Spectrum Disorder — an inability to socialize with other people, recognize social clues and not say the wrong things at the wrong time.

The first thing I would recommend is for young Tahl to find a safe harbor, such as the Covenant House, where he will be safe, eat properly and get adequate sleep for a few days. For most patients, safety, food and sleep will immediately enhance their well-being even before starting psycho-therapy. Sleep deprivation alone produces hallucinations and even psychosis.

I would begin therapy by asking young Tahl: "What are your best hopes for being here, in therapy?"

And young Tahl would respond: "To become a table tennis champion and live in my own apartment."

Successful therapy is rooted in an understanding of what a client wants his or her life to become.

Then, together, young Tahl and psychotherapist Tahl would explore his anxieties, try to manage his cognitive distortions and find day-to-day coping solutions. Finally, we would focus on how to relate better to ourselves and to others.

I would also encourage young Tahl to continue playing table tennis as much as possible. There's something special about this sport that makes it quite therapeutic. It is both physically and mentally challenging at the same time, which is why it normally takes newcomers months to get to the point where they can maintain a rally. And because table tennis requires full concentration, that in itself provides an important respite from problems and anxieties. A time to rest and restore.

* * *

I remember the night I was coming out of the J Train at 111th Street and saw an elderly woman being robbed on the subway platform by a young guy with a knife. When the woman refused to hand over her purse, he slashed her arm, grabbed her purse and ran. I made sure she was okay, and then ran after the kid up the steps to the street above. I never would have caught him, but some cops who happened to be coming around a nearby corner tackled him. "Why were you chasing him?" one of the cops asked me. I told them why and they arrested him.

I'll never forget the fear and hurt I saw in that woman's eyes. Emotions that had been a big part of my own childhood. Feelings she and I shared. I saw my own pain in her eyes, our shared human frailty. Inflicting pain on others was something I just couldn't and wouldn't do — unless I was attacked.

That's why I never hurt people who didn't try to hurt me. Why I didn't threaten anyone with violence unless they attacked me? And though I did steal food and clothing from stores, I never held anyone up at the point of a knife or a pistol. When some of the kids I hung out with on the streets started robbing people with weapons, I opted out.

But I did start carrying a big steak knife. I never pulled it on anyone unless they threatened me with a weapon. I used it to discourage other people from attacking me.

After a couple of years of sleeping on subway trains, I graduated to sleeping on the rooftops or in the basements of apartment buildings I'd break into. The seats on subway trains are designed for sitting upright, not sleeping, and every stop is an opportunity for would-be attackers to corner and rob you. Rooftops and basements were safer, though I had my share of violent escapades there, too.

One night, I woke up in the basement of an apartment building to find the super's son molesting my girlfriend who was sleeping next to me. He was a very big guy, but I fought him off until his father came and ushered us out of the building.

Sleeping

Finding a comfortable place to sleep is a major problem for homeless people. The seats on subway cars, as I just mentioned, are designed for sitting upright, not lying down. And when you're sleeping on a rooftop or in a basement room, it's usually on concrete. I was in almost constant pain because of the bone tumors in my lower spine and a lack of a decent bed to sleep on.

Many homeless people sleep in city-run shelters or in the tunnels of Grand Central Station, but I never felt comfortable or safe sleeping in either place. So, like a lot of homeless people, I often went without sleep for two or more days. The only really restful sleep I had during my life on the streets was on the beach in the summers.

Sleep deprivation creates all kinds of serious problems, physical and psychological. Which explains in part the high incidence of mental illness among homeless people.

Eating

During my first year on the streets, I regularly dined at Sizzler's, a steak house on 63rd Drive on Queens Boulevard. The restaurant's buffet area had an exit door leading to the street. I'd wait until somebody came out of that door, rush into the buffet area, scoop food into brown paper bags or my backpack, and hightail it back into the street. I did get caught a few times, but never arrested. Eventually, the manager and I had a heart-to-heart discussion. "Look," he said, "you can't come in here anymore. It's not good for our business. It makes our customers uncomfortable." After that little talk, I knew they would be looking out for me, so I had to remove Sizzler's from my list of preferred food sources.

Supermarkets were a plentiful source of sustenance. I'd walk into the shop, throw food into my backpack, and casually stroll out of the supermarket as if I'd changed my mind about buying groceries. A good sandwich kept me going for a full day. I got caught many times and put out on the street. The first time I was nabbed was in a supermarket on Jamaica Avenue and 85th Street. The manager was very aggressive physically, but he didn't call the police. He threw me out of the store and told me to never come back. Fortunately, there were plenty of other supermarkets in New York City with equally nutritious sandwiches.

Amazingly, I was never detained and arrested when I was caught stealing food. Managers did their job and kicked me out of their restaurants and supermarkets, but they never called the police. Perhaps they were uncomfortable about locking up a homeless 5-foot 3-inch teenager. Maybe their encounter with a hungry kid like me put them in touch with our shared humanity.

Covenant House on 15th Street and Ninth Avenue and a church on Atlantic Avenue were good sources of occasional hot meals. Sometimes a friend would invite me to his house for dinner, or my sister Maja would sneak me into our dad's house, where she was living, give me some food and let me sleep under her bed. Eventually, our father found out Maja was sheltering me and kicked her out of the house, too.

I was hungry most of my time on the street. But I never came close to starving or eating out of garbage cans. Food is incredibly plentiful in our country.

Not long after I left home for the streets, a friend at the South Queen's Boy's Club invited me to his house for Christmas dinner. He had five brothers, so it was a big family gathering, something I'd never experienced at my home when I was growing up. His mother gave me a book as a present. That evening is one of my best teenage memories.

Personal Hygiene

Occasionally, I showered at a YMCA or the South Queens Boys Club. But there were long periods of time, weeks and sometimes months, when I went without bathing. Dandruff was a constant companion. Lice was never a problem. I would deliberately walk in the rain to cleanse myself, and occasionally wash my clothes at a laundromat.

I don't think I smelled bad because my fellow passengers didn't move to other subway cars to get away from me. Most of them didn't even realize I was homeless unless they saw me trying to get some sleep.

Finding a public bathroom at subway stations was never a problem. Alleyway toilets were just as plentiful.

I didn't need to see a doctor or go to a hospital for almost 20 years. My daily four-hour table tennis practice kept me in decent physical health and shape.

Clothing

Clothing wasn't a problem. Church giveaways were a good source of clean shirts and jackets. And if I needed new sneakers and socks, which was often, I'd shoplift them at sporting goods stores. I'd walk into a store, try on a pair of sneakers, put my old sneakers in the shoe box, and walk out wearing the new pair. I got caught once stealing sneakers at Modell's in the Queens Center mall. They detained me for quite a few hours, but didn't arrest me.

I was also caught stealing clothing at Macy's. I went there with a couple of street friends: Carlos, a Spanish-speaking kid whose family lived in Woodhaven, and Ryan, a tall 6'5" Irish kid. For some stupid reason, the two of them were hellbent on creating a ruckus by dropping glass objects on the floor. I tried to put some distance between me and them, but the cops showed up and took us all into a back room. Ryan didn't like most people, particularly policemen. So he bad-mouthed the cops, and they retaliated by punching the hell out of him. It was one of the most savage beatings I've ever seen. Afterwards, they just let us go. I guess we were not worth the paperwork our arrest would generate.

Friendship

I made a lot of friends on the street. Juan was my best friend. We slept on the trains for a couple of years before he convinced me we'd be safer sleeping on the rooftops of apartment buildings we broke into. Juan was two years younger than me. He didn't get along with his family who lived in New Jersey. He didn't get along with most people.

Juan was even angrier than Ryan. If somebody looked at him when we were on the trains or in the streets, he'd attack them. He often got into fights with other homeless people. I was always trying to calm him down, keep him out of trouble.

Where Juan and I parted company was robbing people on the streets at knife- or gunpoint. Like I already said, I didn't mind stealing from restaurants or stores. But not from individuals. Juan understood we were different and never tried to involve me in armed robbery.

Many people don't understand the difference between shoplifting and robbing someone on the street. The main distinction for me was that the former was impersonal. It didn't involve threatening to harm somebody if they didn't hand over their money or possessions. It didn't involve violence or the threat of violence. I had enough of that fending off people trying to take my backpack and any money they mistakenly thought I had.

Juan also understood that I didn't do drugs or sell them. I tried marijuana once, and didn't like it. Same with cocaine. My drug of choice was table tennis. It kept me focused. It was something I did exceptionally well every day from 4-9 p.m. at the South Queens Boys Club. It was the perfect escape from the many stresses of homelessness — fighting, hunger, sleeplessness.

If I got arrested and jailed for a serious crime, like armed robbery or drug dealing, that could end my one and only real ambition in life at that time — becoming a world-class table tennis player. Vinny Cartagena, the South Queens Boys Club program director and my very first table tennis coach, had formed a league involving many of New York City's youth clubs. So I was competing regularly against very good players, and more than holding my own. My ambition was becoming a reality!

A recent photo of me, Vinny and Sean at the
South Queens Boys and Girls Club of America

53

One of Juan's street friends, Nefti, got into big trouble selling drugs, not with the cops but with a big time dealer. The dealer gave him an 8 Ball of cocaine to sell which is an eighth of an ounce or 3.5 grams. Nefti didn't understand he was supposed to divide the cocaine into eight $10.00 packets. Instead, he sold the entire 8 Ball for $10.00. The dealer dangled him by his feet off the roof of a tall building until he agreed to sell enough drugs to reimburse the dealer.

Ryan also got into trouble with a dealer who smacked him around pretty badly. Watching that beating reminded me of my father who would suddenly and without warning attack me. We feared the drug dealers much like I feared my father. They were older guys. Nefti and Ryan were just kids hustling loose change.

I ran into Juan a couple of years ago at his brother's wedding. He's doing okay. Working in construction. Married with two kids. He got his life together. He straightened out. He's driving a BMW. He asked me if I thought he made a mistake by spending all his money on a car. I didn't have the heart to tell him that it might not have been the best move.

Another street friend, Marty, was a magician who mentored me in the art of shoplifting. Our main targets were the electronics shops in Chinatown where the merchandise hangs on clothes lines. We'd walk into a store in Chinatown, Marty would point to something and ask the clerk how much it cost, while stealing something else with his other hand. Misdirection was his forte. We'd walk out of the shops with small radios and other electronic devices that we'd sell on the street.

Making money was the goal. My street friends would do anything to make money. And though I drew the line at armed robbery and drug dealing, they were the only friends I had. Today, I can afford to be more discriminating.

* * *

When I was 16 and still homeless, I decided to visit my father. When I walked into his house, he got very angry and threatened to fight me. But he hesitated. He knew I was different. No longer terrified by aggressive grown men, I stood up to him and didn't show fear, and he stood down. He was afraid of me!

Around the same time, I ran into one of my former school bullies. We were walking on the same side of the street, and when he recognized me, he started walking towards me with an angry expression on his face. When he got closer, he realized I wasn't the same meek kid he used to torment, but it was too late for him to avoid me. I punched him so hard he dropped to the ground instantly. And then I kicked him a few times. Walking away, I actually felt bad about hurting him.

* * *

So I was living two lives. A homeless teenager living on the street, and a member of the South Queens Boys Club. Unlike Juan, I belonged to a community who shared a passion for a competitive sport, a community built on healthy relationships. That's probably why I didn't share his and Ryan's anger towards people in general, why I never disliked other people and wanted to harm them, why I didn't do drugs or hold up people with a weapon.

* * *

Over the next two years, up until my 16th birthday, I played at the South Queens Boys and Girls Club every day. When the other kids went home for dinner, the club's director, Leo Compton, helped me push the table against a wall so I could continue playing, Forrest Gump-style, against the wall.

Leo knew I couldn't go home for supper because I was homeless. He also knew I wasn't going to school, and that we were breaking the club's rule that barred truants from club membership. Despite our contentious relationship and frequent arguments, Leo made a big exception for me.

* * *

In 2012, shortly after Leo retired, he told Hillel Kuttler of *The Times of Israel*, "My rule at the club was: You have to go to school. But with Tahl, it was different. He would've been lost if he didn't have something to grow with and build his confidence. He had that with table tennis."

"The ball and paddle would just click, and he could spend an hour straight without missing the ball at all," Compton said. "Then I bought a machine for him that could hit the ball to him at angles.

"Tahl would have been lost if he didn't have table tennis."

Leo also told the reporter that I was troubled by the incessant bullying of kids who were bigger than me and was kicked out of school because of the constant fighting. He also said he often tried to patch things up between me and my mother.

"I'd say (to Tahl), 'You can't ride the trains. It's dangerous. You don't have to love [your mother], but you have to respect her."

Leo ran the club for 26 years. After he died in early 2023, his family sent me a card. "Leo adored and loved you," they wrote on the card. I was surprised to hear that, but it felt good.

* * *

The table tennis program at the South Queens Boys' Club grew rapidly. As we improved as players, we became closer as a group and stopped fighting each other. Then, in 1990, the club's program director, Vinny Cartagena, set up a billiards and table tennis league involving six other youth clubs throughout New York City.

We got killed the first year of league competition. In the second year, we won the league championship.

Vinny also employed a United States Table Tennis Federation certified coach, Alex Freberg, to run the table tennis program at the South Queens Boys Club. Freeberg, who also coached at the Lost Battalion Club, introduced structured training and drills that helped us become much better players.

Many of my lifelong friends, like Jerry Vasquez, were kids from other clubs who I competed against in Vinny's league competition.

In 1990, Vinny took two players from our club, Glen Brown and David Fernandez to train with the U.S. Olympic table tennis team at the Olympic Training Center in Colorado Springs. That, more than anything else, convinced us we were future table tennis champions.

The Lost Battalion Hall

The Lost Battalion Hall in 2017. Constructed in 1939
as a firing range and drill hall, it became a New York
City Parks recreational center in 1962.

In late 1991, I got into a major confrontation at the South Queens
Boys Club. Leo and Vinny wrongly accused me of swearing in the
club, and I refused to do the 10 pushups penalty. That's when I
started playing regularly at the Lost Battalion Club in Rego Park,
New York, along with three friends from the South Queens Boys
Club: David Fernandez, Glenn Brown and Santo Vasquez.

The teenagers who played at the LBC were mostly white
local kids with a smattering of Black, Brown, East Asian and Russian kids. All of them were highly rated 2100 to 2300 players,
much higher than my intermediate rating of 1400.

Once again, I was relegated to the bottom of the pack and openly ridiculed by the other kids and some of the adults who worked at the LBC: "You're no good," they told me. "Don't play on this table." "You really should give up this game." They were not happy playing a beginner like me, but I kept coming back, kept playing matches.

* * *

There's a time in your development as a table tennis player when you move up to a higher level and take losses. Some kids just can't manage defeats. They just give up. I never have. I've always pushed through to the next level. Giving up was never an option.

* * *

The Lost Battalion Club had a winner-take-all set-up, which meant if you kept winning matches, you never had to sit down. So if I lost a match at 4:00 pm, when the club opened, I wouldn't get another match until 6:30 pm. I really couldn't compete against these highly skilled players. The only points I won were either net cords or edge skimmers. Usually, I lost games without winning a single point, 21-to-0.

While I sat there for hours waiting for another turn to play, I closely observed each player's weaknesses — the speed, spin and placement that challenged them. I focused not on beating them, but instead on how I could make play difficult for them. Doing that relieved the bad feeling of losing. I had a strategy, a plan that would succeed no matter how many games I lost. And I knew, deep down, if my technique continued to get better, my understanding of their weaknesses would eventually transform me into one of the LBC's better players.

A year and a half after joining the Lost Battalion Club, I was the best player there. So much better that the LBC instituted a win-three-match sit-down rule so that I didn't hog a table for the entire six hours the club was open. My winning made some of the other players very unhappy. They just couldn't accept losing to me, a small kid with limited physical movement. A few tried to trash-talk me out of my game, but that didn't work because I disliked losing even more than they did.

Six months later, when I was eighteen, I realized that if I was to continue improving as a table tennis player, I needed to compete against tougher competition. So I began competing in tournaments certified by the United States Association of Table Tennis. The prize money, though puny compared to that of other sports, came in very handy.

Ill-Gainful Employment

My shoplifting career ended when I became friends with Carlos who was working for a department store and stealing the credit card numbers of the store's customers. That was less risky than shoplifting. Carlos and I bought merchandise on the phone using stolen credit card numbers and had the goods delivered to postal boxes. We then sold the merchandise to friends and people on the street. We also sold credit card numbers to other thieves for $100 for each card.

I stopped stealing credit card numbers when it became a federal offense and Carlos was arrested and faced serious jail time. In fact, I stopped stealing altogether and started working for telemarketing companies that were much better at ripping off people than I could ever be — something it took me a little while to figure out.

I was sixteen when I got my first telemarketing job working for a medical supply company. I called people up, told them we wanted to send them a nice gift at cost, and wrote down their credit card information. The company then shipped them a gift worth about $20 or less — often a cheap watch —and charged their card up to $490. If they purchased medical supplies, the company marked up the cost by 800 percent. I was manning my phone when government agents raided the office and arrested the company's managers.

My next telemarketing job was for the Magnum Vending Corporation which was selling pizza vending machines at $8,000 a pop. I still remember the first line of the company's eight-page script that we telemarketers read to prospective buyers over the phone: "Vending is a $26 billion industry, and two-thirds of that money is earned by small vendors working only a few hours a week servicing their machines." I sold many vending machines to people who couldn't resist the prospect of making easy money, vending machines they never received. Once again, government agents stormed into my workplace and handcuffed the company's officers. "20/20" aired an expose of the company's scam, and the parent company based in Florida was successfully sued by the Fair Trade Commission and ordered to pay a fine of $31 million.

Sterling Who's Who was my next telemarketing job of record. I sold exclusive memberships to individuals who paid $749.00 to $25,000 for the privilege of having their name listed in the company's publication of community and business leaders. In appreciation for their membership, the company gifted them with a beautiful plaque worth three or four dollars. We telemarketers used to joke around that the only real qualification for inclusion in this very exclusive listing of prominent people was to have a credit card in your name. Over 60,000 individuals fell for this scam before the government shut it down.

Compared to shoplifting and credit card theft, telemarketing for companies swindling the public was a cake walk. I was good at these jobs. I was good at speaking, and I was good at sales. I was so good that my friends told me I sounded like a sales professional.

My only other means of making money, other than tournament prize money, was hustling people at table tennis clubs and at colleges where the level of play is low. Sometimes I would sit in a chair and play people for money. Later on, I began giving table tennis lessons for $10-an-hour.

Work was simply a means of earning enough money to support my table tennis career. It wasn't until I became a social worker and interacted with people needing help that work became interesting to me.

Education

In 1990, when I was 16, I decided to take the test for a General Education Development degree because I thought a GED would help me get a good paying job. So I enrolled in the GED program at John Adams High School in Ozone Park, Queens, and took the practice test. I failed it miserably. Just what you'd expect from somebody who dropped out of school after a few weeks in the 9th grade.

"Look, it's going to take you two years to prepare for the GED," I was told. "You don't have the skills to pass this exam."

I wasn't about to wait two years. "You know what," I replied, "I'm going to take the exam anyway. If I fail, then I'll come back."

Back then, nobody could tell me what I could or couldn't do. When I began playing table tennis, many of the other players and even a few coaches told me I was wasting my time, I'd never become a skilled competitor. Well, they were wrong. So why should I listen to anyone's opinions of my ability to succeed in anything, including education? There was nothing I couldn't accomplish if I put my mind to it. And even if I wanted to take that two-year GED prep course, I didn't have the money to pay the enrollment fee or buy textbooks.

So I spent the next few weeks studying for the GED in libraries and Barnes & Noble bookstore cafes. and when I retook the exam, I passed it with a score just two points above failing. I was lucky. The only reason I passed, I now realize, was back then the GED test did not include advanced mathematics and was therefore much easier.

The other reason I passed that exam was the love of reading instilled in me by my educated parents. Even when I was homeless and living on the street, I managed to spend many mornings in public libraries and bookstore cafes reading books on a fairly wide range of subjects from Eastern Philosophy to the Art of War before rushing off to practice table tennis at the Lost Battalion Club.

Two years later, I enrolled in the Adult Collegiate Program at the City University of New York's Queens College. I took 27 credits, ended up with a 1.7 GPA, was put on probation for a semester, and then kicked out of school. Two years later, I reenrolled at Queens College and flunked out a second time.

The people running the GED program at John Adams High School were right. I needed to go back to school, all the way back to the 9th grade, and acquire the foundation skills of a grade school education.

* * *

Defiance shielded my self-image from bullying schoolmates, abusive parents and trash-talking table tennis competitors. It also sometimes deafened me to the sound advice of well-meaning people. Defiance was definitely a two-edged sword. At least for me.

* * *

By the time I enrolled at LaGuardia, homelessness had taken a toll on my emotional health. Years of sleep deprivation and constant combat led to stress-related hallucinations. Convinced that non-human monsters with evil intentions were following me, I would jump off a subway car and run on the tracks to the next station. I also had conversations with people who didn't exist. It all seemed very real to me.

Fortunately, these hallucinations were short-lived and lasted less than six months. But while they were part of my life, learning math, writing school papers, and studying for exams at LaGuardia were impossible tasks. Even reading for pleasure, for the first time in my life, was difficult.

* * *

Years later, while working at an outpatient psychiatric center with clients who experienced similar thought disorders, I realized what I had experienced was a loss of reality. Life circumstances that are detrimental to our emotional, physical and spiritual wellbeing can have a damaging effect on how we perceive our world. I believe these frightening hallucinations are escape hatches or coping mechanisms.

What saved me was the one constant in my life — my overarching commitment to becoming a top table tennis player and not do anything that would interfere with that goal, like doing drugs. And belonging to a social group of like-minded kids who shared a passion for the sport of table tennis. I was not entirely alone. I belonged somewhere. Unlike most of my street friends.

* * *

In 1995, my twin sister Maja, who always looked after me whenever she could, got a job and rented an apartment in Queens for both of us to share. Our father had kicked her out of his house when he discovered she was letting me sleep under her bed during cold winter nights and sneaking me food to eat. Now, finally, both of us had a place to live where we felt safe. And although we sometimes couldn't pay our utility bills, and had to live without heat or hot water, that didn't seem like much of an inconvenience compared to sleeping on subway trains and rooftops. Or, in Maja's case, living with an angry, physically abusive father.

* * *

Later that same year, at a tournament hosted by the Westfield Table Tennis Club in New Jersey, I met Chris Lehman, a U.S. Paralympic team coach. Chris asked me about my physical disabilities, and when I told him about the benign bone tumors that limit my arm and leg movement, he encouraged me to try out for the country's Paralympic team.

I was twenty at the time and just beginning to accept the reality of my being physically disabled — a reality previously buried under a ton of self-denial. My physical disabilities were slowly worsening. I had lost much of the flexibility in my right wrist. So the timing of Chris' suggestion was fortuitous, and I soon went through the process of qualifying for Paralympic classification.

* * *

Table tennis was included in the first Paralympic Games in Rome in 1960, 28 years before the sport debuted in the Olympics. All competitors were in wheelchairs. Standing para competitors did not compete until the 1976 Toronto Paralympics.

Today, Para table tennis athletes compete in eleven classes according to their degree of physical or mental disability. Wheelchair players are in classes one to five; players able to compete while standing are in the higher classes of six to ten, and competitors who are intellectually impaired are in class 11. The lower the number, the greater the impact a para-athlete's disability has on his or her ability to compete.

The first step in becoming a Paralympic athlete is being assigned to a classification group following a physical examination. The person tasked with vetting my qualification as a Paralympic athlete was Sharon Brooks. Shortly after I received my classification, Sharon raised enough money through her synagogue in Lebanon, New Jersey, to pay my way to the 1995 U.S. National Championships where I competed in both Paralympic and able-bodied player events. I am one of the hundreds of Paralympic athletes who received financial aid from Sharon over the years. Following my early successes at Para tournaments, I was upgraded from Class 7 to Class 9.

* * *

I competed in my first para tournament, the Paralympic Games in Atlanta, in 1996. With former world champion Mitchell Seidenfeld as a teammate, I won the bronze medal in the team event, and, to everybody's surprise, also won the gold medal in Class 7 singles.

Me competing in a 1996 Paralympic event.
(Photo by Mal Anderson)

Going into the gold medal match against the German player, Jochen Wollmert, I thought I needed a leg up. Wollmert had beaten me in both the group and team events. So I resorted to a bit of trash-talking, a dialect popular among the kids I grew up with.

"Why did you bomb Pearl Harbor?" I asked in a loud voice while we were warming up for our singles match, hoping that my historically inaccurate remark would put Wollmert off his game. Wollmert and his German team members were visibly upset by my silly question. So were the mostly American spectators who during the match cheered on the German player to beat me, their fellow countrymen.

The jeering of my fellow Americans didn't bother me a bit. Back then, winning was everything. Nothing else really mattered. Opponents were enemies to be vanquished. Obstacles to be jumped over on my way to victory. They were not friends. They were enemies. They stood between me and the championships I was destined to win. Whatever it took to beat them, including trash-talking, was fair.

Wollmert was an amazing player. His disability gave him great problems with his forehand stroke, but his backhand was world-class. So he played most points with his stronger backhand, even balls most players would return with their forehands.

With the help of my teammate Mitch Seidenfeld, I put together a winning strategy. If I could prevent Wollmert from launching a full backhand attack, I could take advantage of his weaker forehand. So I began the match by hitting short and medium balls to his stronger backhand — which his opponents normally avoided. Then I followed up with shots to his weaker forehand. The unorthodoxy of my game plan unnerved him, and his confidence waned.

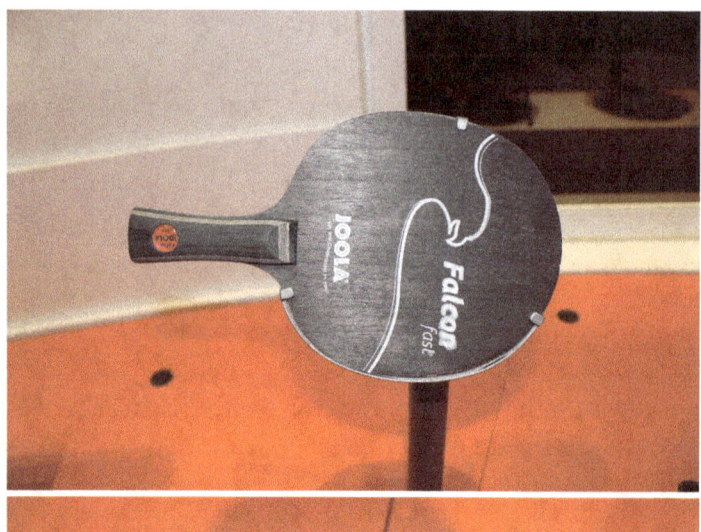

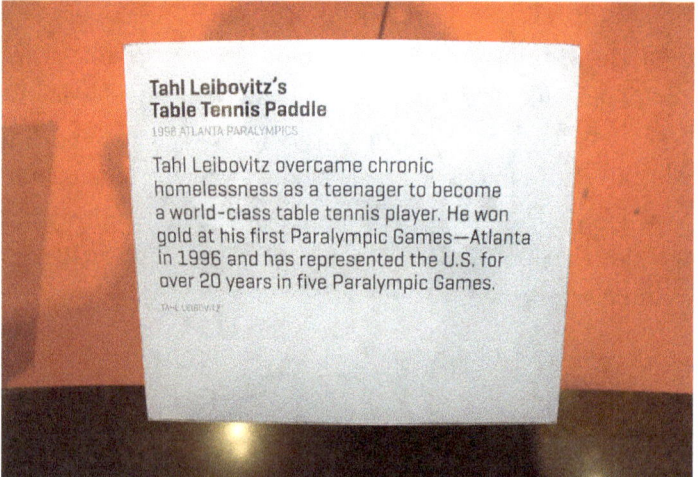

**Tahl Leibovitz's
Table Tennis Paddle**
1996 ATLANTA PARALYMPICS

Tahl Leibovitz overcame chronic
homelessness as a teenager to become
a world-class table tennis player. He won
gold at his first Paralympic Games—Atlanta
in 1996 and has represented the U.S. for
over 20 years in five Paralympic Games.

TAHL LEIBOVITZ

The paddle I used to win the 2019 Parapan American Games
and qualify for the 2020 Paralympics Games. It's now on display
at the USOPC Museum in Colorado Springs, Colorado.

Wollmert went on to win many Paralympic gold medals and become what many consider the best standing para table tennis player ever. But on that day, my trash talking and game strategy prevailed.

Jochen Wollmert, holding up one of the many gold medals he has won in both team and individual Paralympic events during the last 32 years.

* * *

I remember playing a match against a highly ranked 2600 player in an able-bodied tournament. Before the match began, without saying a word to me, he moved my table tennis racquet and bag off from the top of the table to underneath the table. I considered this behavior to be an obvious attempt to intimidate me, show me who was really in control of our upcoming match. Before I could stop myself, I cursed him out. "Don't touch my things or I'll kill you," I screamed. It wasn't the best course of action, but at least it was a reaction.

He was right. I was intimidated by him, fearful of playing someone so much higher ranked than myself. But I didn't want him to know that. I wanted him to see me as an opponent who was confident of winning the match. Which I was. And always am.

My projected self-confidence had a positive effect on both my opponent and me, and I ended up winning that match.

Years later, we met in another match. During a rally, I mishit a ball that just missed his head. "Don't do that again, or I'll kill you," he yelled. Table tennis players have long memories.

* * *

After starting college in 2006, my view of opponents began to soften. I no longer saw myself as just a professional table tennis player. I was also a college student. Table tennis had to move aside to make room for education. Getting a college degree was every bit as important to me as winning tournaments. My life was becoming more balanced.

Table tennis opponents, it finally occurred to me, were really mirror images of myself, competitors doing the best they could to win. They were not enemies. They were partners in the sport of table tennis. Slowly, I began to form friendships with other players.

But even today, during a match, the killer instinct occasionally roars back and I erupt in anger. I'm definitely a work-in-progress.

* * *

The last time I saw Zack was when I returned from playing in the 1995 USA National Championships in Las Vegas. I was depressed by my mediocre performance at the tournament. Zack called and cheered me up quite a bit, and we got together at the local diner. It was good to have a friend like him.

"The tournament was a learning experience," he told me. "You will get better."

Zach was from Pakistan. He was a bit older and taller than me, in exceptionally good physical shape, and very high energy. Zach loved to talk. He had a degree in Chemistry from New York University, but never wanted to work as a chemist. After our practice sessions at the Lost Battalion Club, we would sit for hours in the Burger King across the street and talk, often about philosophy. He was wise. He was a mentor.

But we were quite different. I was focused on table tennis. Zack was focused on his relationship with his girlfriend. Zack lived in rented rooms. I lived on the subway or the roofs of apartment buildings. Yet we were remarkably close friends, and table tennis practice partners.

I remember having lunch with him at the Burger King restaurant when a couple of teenagers tried to steal his Walkman while he was in the bathroom. Zack and I fought them off and recovered his Walkman. He could fight, too.

This was one of Zack's easier battles. When Zack was ten, he walked into his mother's bedroom and found her hanging from a rope. He carried a little piece of that horrible experience with him everywhere he went. You could feel it in him.

After Zack stopped playing table tennis, he would occasionally drop off a handwritten letter for me at the Lost Battalion Club. "Are you okay?" he wrote. "I am worried about you." He was a devoted friend.

Five or six years later, after I'd become a top player, I thought he would like to hear that. The only contact information I had was his father's telephone number. Late one night, I called him up. I told his father I used to play table tennis with his son and that we'd been good friends. "I'd like to get back in touch with him," I said.

"Zack is dead," his father said. "He hung himself a few years ago."

I didn't know how to respond. I was silent. I did not know what to say. His father hung up a few seconds later. I never called him back. Never tried to find out more about Zack's suicide. Probably because I wanted to remember Zack the way he was when we were practicing and hanging out. Not when he was hanging from the end of a rope. It was painful to lose a close friend.

* * *

Years later, after I became a licensed psychotherapist, I worked with a client who reminded me of Zack. He had some traumatic experiences as a child, and when he was 16 years old, he hung himself and was clinically dead for ten minutes. He became my patient shortly after his suicide attempt, and during the next two months, we were able to connect his personal values to how he wanted to live his life — a methodology we psychotherapists call the foundation of Existential Psychotherapy. Today he is doing quite well.

* * *

In 1996, while in Florida competing in the U.S. Open, I visited my maternal grandfather, Simon, who was in a hospital. "I have about four days to live, give or take a few hours," he told me." He then yanked out the drips, got out of bed, and walked around the facility. Death was no stranger to him. Nothing to fear.

"When the Nazis did a culling," he told me, "They always lined up people according to height, and then selected the tallest for extermination. That's why I was spared when they killed my seven brothers in Poland, and why I survived Auschwitz. I was always at the end of the line. Always the shortest. Sometimes I wish I would have been anything but last."

How could I feel sorry for myself knowing what my grandfather endured? How could I not admire his mental fortitude and strength of character? Maybe I had inherited some of his toughness? Maybe we had more in common than our shared height of five-feet three-inches?

* * *

Playing in the 1997 Maccabiah Games was an incredibly special experience. Until that visit, my being Jewish was something the school bullies who called me a kike cared more about than I did. Religion just wasn't part of my childhood. I wasn't ashamed of being a Jew. It was just something that really didn't matter to me, or to my parents. Now, in Israel, back in my birth country as a professional table tennis competitor, I felt part of something larger than myself, something to be proud about. Standing up to my anti-Semitic classmates, defiantly rejecting their attempt to make me feel inferior, now made even more sense.

The only negative experience of that visit to Israel was the collapse of the Maccabiah bridge, a temporary footbridge over the Yarkon River in Tel Aviv, during the opening ceremony. The collapse killed four and injured more than 60 athletes and delegates from Australia.

* * *

My success as a table tennis professional got a jump start in 1998 when I played in my first major tournament, the New York State Championships at the Champion Ping-Pong Club in Jackson Heights, Queens. I had won a gold medal at the 1996 Paralympic Games and now I wanted to battle the best able-bodied players.

The Champion Ping-Pong Club was on Roosevelt Avenue underneath the elevated No.7 subway tracks. Hookers and drug dealers lined the streets. If you wanted crack, this was the place to get it, though it was very possible you'd be robbed by gunpoint before or after you made the deal.

Columbian drug gangs ruled the neighborhood. Crime was rampant.

Bad neighborhoods didn't scare me. If I could survive living and fighting on the subway for most of my teenage years, there was nothing in Jackson Heights I couldn't handle. I was indestructible, almost immortal — an intoxicating feeling that was, of course, irrational.

Walking into the tournament hall, I ran into one of the coaches from the Lost Battalion Club, Errol Young. Errol had refused to coach me at the LBC because he didn't think I had what it takes to get really good at the sport. Today, he sang a different tune. "You going to do great today," he said.

Errol was quite a character. He told us kids at the LBC that when he hooked a fish, he told the fish: "I'm not going to kill you if you bring other fish back here where I'm fishing." He also bragged about single-handedly lifting the engine out of his car without a hoist when it needed fixing. He was a natural-born storyteller.

Although I had achieved good results as a paralympic athlete, my performance at able-bodied tournaments was mediocre. Walking into the competition halls, I felt like a pretender who was not ready to compete at the highest level of the sport. I expected to lose. "Why should this tournament be any different?" I thought to myself.

After I won my semifinal match against Coach Lee, a highly rated player who before emigrating to the U.S had trained China's national team — the world's dominant table tennis competitors — I bumped into Coach Young again. "You're going to win it all," he told me. "You're going to beat Abass."

Coach Young had a reputation for being a very persuasive match motivator, and though I was puzzled by his newfound belief in my ability, what he said to me at that tournament had a positive effect, perhaps on a subconscious level, because I did fight my way through to the singles final against one of the world's top players, the Nigerian Abass Ukan.

Abass, like all of my able-bodied opponents, dwarfed my 5-feet 3-inches frame and outweighed me by at least 49 lbs. Then ranked No.5 in the U.S. and one of New York City's most in-demand table tennis coaches, Abass' ability to spin short and mid-court topspin returns was formidable.

He was known for his warm and winning personality, love of joking around. He was obviously a person who enjoyed life. What happened after our match ended was definitely out-of-character.

During our match, a large crowd of onlookers gathered behind the court barriers. Most were cheering me on, the underdog. Eric Cardona, a young player a year or two older than me, was particularly loud and vociferous in his support. As the match progressed, I could see Abass was becoming increasingly annoyed by Eric's loud cheering for his opponent.

In the fifth and deciding game, with Abass up 16-14, I decided to switch strategy. Up to that point, I had been playing to Abass' strength — short and mid-court topspin returns. Now, instead of re-turning his serve short or to mid-court, I cut a heavy underspin return long to his backhand, which he missed. On his next serve, I pushed deep to his forehand, and though he was able to spin the ball back, I blocked his ball off the short bounce for a winner.

The match was tied at 16 all when I realized he was feeling the pressure of possibly losing to a much lower-rated player. So I became extremely aggressive, hitting chop blocks and smashes.

My strategy worked, and I managed to win the fifth and deciding game, 21-19, against a player who was at that time much more skilled than me. Abass was so distraught at losing the match, he threw his water bottle at Eric and tried to punch him before being restrained by the crowd.

Coach Young, who recently passed away, played a key part in that triumph. The coach who a few years earlier told me I'd never get good at the sport, played a crucial part in helping me win my first major able-bodied tournament.

My victory against Abass changed everything. While there was still much about the game I had to learn, never again did I doubt my ability to compete against the sport's elite competitors. Never again did I assume an opponent would beat me, no matter how much higher rated he or she was. This is the mindset of every successful sports competitor. The belief that on a given day, you can beat anyone.

* * *

I met Sean O'Neill at the 2002 World Championships in Taiwan. Sean told me he was thinking about coaching the U.S. Paralympic Team. I had skipped the 2000 Paralympic Games because of a personality clash with one of the para players, and was actually thinking about retiring from the sport. Competitive table tennis was just not enjoyable for me anymore, though I had little idea of what else I could do.

At the U.S. National Championships in Las Vegas, Sean and I practiced together and I won five straight games. Although Sean retired 15 years earlier, he was still a very strong player. During his prime, he was a five-time U.S. Champion and a two-time Olympian.

Sean O'Neill in his prime

Sean convinced me to come back and train for the 2004 Paralympics. "I'll help you become an even better player," he said. "Together, we'll do the best we can." I agreed. It was one of the smartest decisions of my young life.

Sean on Coaching Paralympic Athletes

My journey into the world of Para Table Tennis began with countless matches against Para players throughout my career. At first, they were merely opponents on the table, and their unique stories remained a mystery to me. That changed in 2002 when I became the Lead Coach for Para Table Tennis under the auspices of the USOC.

In this new capacity, I delved into the intricacies of both wheelchair and standing disabled table tennis. What struck me profoundly was the diversity among these athletes – their distinct styles, personalities and stages in life. It quickly became evident that treating each player with unwavering respect and providing unwavering support, while simultaneously pushing them to excel as athletes, was essential to our mutual success.

There's a deep personal satisfaction in being fully committed to helping my players give their all in every match. It's a commitment recognized not only by my athletes but also by opposing coaches.

Win or lose, regardless of the disparity in skill levels or the challenges we face, we fight. We persevere. As I continue to work with local Para players, I hold onto the hope that one day, they too will pass on this spirit to the next generation of Team USA athletes. Together, we will see the Stars and Stripes proudly adorning the podium.

Sean's coaching was different than anything I had previously experienced. Most coaches focus on what you should do. Sean talks about what you shouldn't do. "Never worry about the results or satisfying other people with your performance," he told me. He also helped me understand that while table tennis competition often resembles life, it really isn't bigger than life itself — a lesson reinforced a few years later by my other para coaches, Stellan and Angie Bengtsson.

Sean's approach to the sport is both meticulous and holistic. Proper sleep and nutrition go hand-in-hand with a healthy attitude toward competition. No other player or coach I know trains harder than Sean, or focuses more on the psychological or mental component of the sport of table tennis.

Mentoring

As we got to know each other better while traveling to tournaments around the world, I realized Sean was not only interested in my success as a table tennis competitor. He was also interested in helping me succeed in life as well. He was much more than a coach; he was also a mentor and father figure. We spent a lot of time discussing the problems I was having outside the tournament halls. If I felt discouraged at school, he encouraged me to carry on and spent hours helping me study and prepare for upcoming exams. If I had a personal problem, he helped me figure out how to resolve it.

Sean applies the same positive approach to coaching. When I lost a match, he helped me understand why I lost, how my opponent attacked my weaknesses, and what weaknesses in the opponent's play I could exploit the next time we competed. Sean taught me information is the key to success, in table tennis and in life.

Sean's mentoring over the last 20 years has had an amazingly positive impact on the person I've become and the life I lead helping others less advantaged than I am. His devotion to me and the Paralympic athletes he trains and coaches is truly inspiring.

Sean's Perspective On Our Partnership

Although often touted as an individual sport, I have always been inspired by table tennis' team dynamics. Underneath the one-on-one showdowns, the captivating duet of doubles, and the enigmatic allure of mixed doubles lies an even richer narrative — the symbiotic partnership of coach and player, an unbreakable alliance that transcends the ordinary.

Drawing from my own days as a player and the privilege of learning under some of table tennis' finest mentors, my transition into coaching carried me into the orbit of esteemed Olympic and Paralympic mentors from around the globe. Borrowing liberally from their treasure trove of wisdom — concepts, ideologies, training methods and techniques — my intellect was captivated by the realm of tactics and sports psychology, the art of strategic prowess, and the mental fortitude needed to outmaneuver adversaries on the grandest stages of the sport.

Within this multifaceted tapestry of shared experience, a singular partnership between me and Tahl emerged over the last twenty-five years, a transformative amalgamation of energies that has propelled both of us towards our very best efforts as coach and competitor. This communion thrives on reciprocity. The insights I observe into Tahl's behavior off the table become the grist of my counsel about what is needed for him to avoid errors on the table.

But the essence of our partnership unfolds on the canvas of competition where our victories and defeats are chronicled. Some, of course, are more memorable than others.

In 2002, the Para World Table Tennis Championships took us to Taiwan City, Taipei, which we affectionately called "Bizarro World." As the Team Leader of the U.S. Paralympic Table Tennis contingent, I needed to jump into the shoes of coach while our athletes battled simul-taneously on different fronts. Tahl's reverence for my past accolades and playing acumen dismissed any inkling of doubt he had about my coaching, even when our perspectives diverged.

"Bizarro World" refers to a competitor's perception of how good they are at table tennis. It is a state of being. Many players think they can just show up and win. World class table tennis requires so much more. Tahl understands the grind and persistence needed to compete successfully. All I ask of my students is that they put in the hard work so they're ready to compete at all levels of the sport.

In the early rounds of the Open event for competitors in Classes 6-10 (10 being those with the least physical disability), Tahl was matched against a Class 10 Chinese player who was celebrated for toppling the very best European players.

When an American locks horns with a Chinese rival in a table tennis match, it usually mirrors the legendary clash of the Washington Generals and the Harlem Globetrotters. During my playing career, as a five-time U.S. Champion, I often wondered if I could win a single point in a match against the great Chinese players Wang Tao or Ma Wenge.

Tahl was not intimidated. Armed with the unique self-confidence of a kid from the streets of New York City, Tahl loudly announced the Chinese player's ability was subpar. This audacity, I realized, could tip the scales in Tahl's favor, especially since he excelled against players with superior ranking, especially left-handed competitors.

The opening game unfolded like a symphony. "I told you this guy sucks," Tahl said after winning the first game.

As the encounter progressed, Tahl continued to defy expectations, and our timeouts evolved into strategic brainstorming sessions. The atmosphere hummed with anticipation among the spectators until Tahl lost the second game, drawing the match even.

"This guy does suck!" Tahl reiterated during the break, obviously frustrated by his failure to win the second game. Steering him away from his perception of his opponent's weakness, I refocused our conversation on how we could win the match.

In the third game, Tahl maneuvered the Chinese player into a defensive game of high lobs in the hope of closing out the match. At match point, Tahl narrowly missed a smash, eliciting a loud palpable sigh of relief from the Chinese contingent.

"Next Point!" I said three times in rapid succession, trying to guide Tahl's thoughts away from frustration to our playbook of seizing the initiative with strategic footwork and prudent choices.

Tahl surged ahead, creating another match point and carving out a fresh opportunity to win the match. Which he did! The euphoria I felt was what I imagined Herb Brooks experienced when his undermanned U.S. hockey team beat the heavily favored Russian team to win a gold medal at the 1980 Olympics.

With this monumental victory, Tahl and I embarked on a journey into the heart of Bizarro World. The triumph over the formidable Chinese rival and Tahl's ensuing comeback victory against Hungary's premier contender stand as keystones of our unshakable partnership.

The essence of our camaraderie mirrors a military unit, where each member propels the collective, shouldering the weight of triumphs and adversities alike. Unity prevails, as we navigate this journey, each carrying the mantle of shared credit and collective endeavor.

My Anger Problem

In 2002, I inherited a fair amount of money from my grandfather Simon's estate, enough to buy a three-bedroom condo duplex in Tudor Village, Queens, New York. The constant stress of homelessness and poverty was finally beginning to recede into the background. I now had a real opportunity to repair my damaged life: get a proper education, mend broken relationships, become an even greater table tennis player. Or so I thought.

But then, yet another malignant symptom of my unhealthy life on the streets bubbled up to the surface, threatening my recovery — the aggressive and quick-to-anger person I'd become.

My girlfriend at the time, an Italian Jewish girl living in Long Island with her mother, told me a friend of hers just released from prison said he was going to kill me because I wasn't treating her right.

That made me incredibly angry. This guy was obviously trying to break up our relationship. He was way out-of-line. And he was challenging me, something I never could ignore.

I was in a very bad place. I wanted to show this guy he didn't scare me. I wanted to threaten him, make him fear me and leave my girlfriend alone. And because he was a hardened criminal just released from prison, I decided I needed an enforcer. So I bought a gun, and started looking for this guy.

A few days later, two policemen showed up at my house. My girlfriend thought I was unstable and had informed the cops I was carrying a gun. "If you give us the firearm," they said, "we won't press charges." As soon as I handed over the weapon, they arrested me and threw me into a holding cell in the Bronx — the so-called "floating jail," an 800-bed prison barge the City shut down in 2023. Sitting in jail looking at a possible prison sentence of up to 25-years for unlawful possession of a firearm got me thinking. Maybe there was a better way to approach life.

Eight days later, I used some of my inheritance from Grandfather Simon to bail myself out and hire a lawyer. My table tennis career, and everything else in life I hoped to accomplish, was in serious jeopardy.

At the hearing, the judge noted that this was my first violent offense and released me on a five-year probation. He also required me to attend anger management classes every week for the next two years.

The class met three times a week from 8:00 - 10:00 a.m. in Queensbridge, the largest public housing project in the U.S., an incredibly bleak and dangerous neighborhood of tall, broken-down apartment buildings — a perfect setting for an end-of-the-world apocalypse movie.

The building where we met was actually on Queens Blvd, the main thoroughfare that separates the gentrified houses of Long Island City from the projects. When I arrived each morning, I would pass through metal detectors and be escorted to the bathroom for a urine test. If I failed the urine test, missed a class, arrived late a second time, or got into a fight during class, I would be immediately thrown back into jail.

I remember my first class. We sat in a circle with the therapist and two security guards, listening to each other's life stories. The guy across from me assaulted a stranger who'd done nothing wrong. The guy next to me beat up his wife. Another classmate almost killed a colleague at work for no good reason. These people belong in a cage, I thought. All they know is violence. For them, every response has to include physical violence.

That's not who I am. I'm different. I don't attack people unless they attack me, or threaten me with violence.

After a few weeks of classes, I fell off my high horse. Listening to the stories of my classmates, getting to know them better, I realized I shared their propensity to violence. I too needed to learn how to respond to life's challenges without resorting to physical violence. Getting a gun to intimidate a guy who told my girlfriend he was going to harm me was a dumb reaction. It didn't solve my girlfriend problems. It just got me into a lot of hot water.

So the anger management classes put me in touch with the intemperate person I'd become. And being on probation helped me straighten myself out. If I got into trouble again, any kind of legal trouble, I'd be thrown back into jail.

The gun episode was a turning point in my life.

* * *

Anger is still a problem. It occasionally surfaces during a match when I miss a shot or misplay a ball. In my earlier playing days, I would demolish my racquet into little broken pieces. Now my goal is to gently place it on the table or floor and quickly walk away, which most times I am able to achieve. And I seldom if ever badmouth my opponent. I can control the anger now, but I can't get rid of it entirely.

* * *

In 2003, I volunteered to work with the American Youth Table Tennis Organization, a nonprofit that runs table tennis programs in New York City's public schools. AYTTO was founded by Ben Nisbett, a lifetime player, certified coach and former USA Table Tennis Executive Director. Most of the kids involved in AYTTO's program go to inner-city schools in New York's poorer neighborhoods in The Bronx, Brooklyn and East New York. Some of them are homeless. Whenever I teach table tennis at one of these schools, I bring food for these kids because I know from personal experience how hungry they are.

Falling in Love - Slowly

In 2004, I met Dawn at the Grandstand Karaoke bar in Maspeth, Queens. I was singing a Bon Jovi song called "Bed of Roses." Afterwards, she complimented me on my singing, and we struck up a conversation. She told me about a book she was reading, The Committed Marriage: A Guide to Finding a Soul Mate and Building a Relationship Through Timeless Biblical Wisdom, written by Rebbetzin Esther Jungreis, a female rabbi. It was obvious to me that Dawn was not interested in conventional dating or premarital sex, and I was okay with that.

Dawn intrigued me. I had been dating since the age of 14, and though some of those relationships were difficult and short-lived, I was always a one-woman guy, always monogamous, always looking for a relationship more harmonious, loving and lasting than what my parents had.

When I met Dawn, I had just ended a four-year relationship and was thinking seriously about marrying and settling down. My goal was to get married by the time I turned 30. So I went on first dates with many women, looking for that perfect fit that would end in matrimony. Three of the 40-to-49 women I dated were potential contenders. None were slam-dunks.

But friendship with Dawn was definitely appealing. She said and did things that amused me. Like sunbathing in the park rather than on the beach, mixing turkey and ham on the same sandwich, and wanting to marry somebody over six feet tall. Every woman I had ever dated was taller than me. And here's a 4-feet 9-inch woman who's half a foot shorter than me wanting to marry a giant. That was more than just amusing. It was challenging.

We started hanging out together. Going to the Cloisters Museum in Upper Manhattan. Taking long walks together, once across Queensborough Bridge. Talking a lot about everything under the sun. Over the next two months, a deep friendship blossomed. The more time we spent together, the more I liked her. She shared my love of reading. She was tough like me, but much calmer and less of a risk-taker. We were a fit.

Dawn never knew her father, or the father of her three Polish-American stepsiblings, and although her family was very poor and homeless for a few nights after a fire destroyed their home, Dawn was blessed with an Italian American mother who loved all her children, was not delusional, and never ran after them brandishing a kitchen knife and screaming "the blood will pour."

After two months of friendship, our relationship transitioned to dating. That's when we started arguing. Some of our arguments generated hurtful words which lead to wounded feelings.

Dawn and I were both damaged by our troubled childhoods, me much more than her. Two repositories of unresolved childhood anger. Her anger over not having a father and being very poor, and my anger towards my abusive, narcissistic father and delusional mother. Without a solid foundation of friendship, our relationship may not have survived these painful arguments.

* * *

"We were both broken. We didn't know how to handle our emotions. We're both survivors, though I think Tahl had it a lot harder than I did. He wasn't loved like I was when we were growing up. I fell in love with him because of his kindness and good heart."

-Dawn Leibovitz

* * *

Doubling with Sean

In March of 2004, Sean O'Neill and I competed in the doubles competition in Washington, D.C., of the U.S. Olympic Trials. Our final match, against Adam Hugh and Han Xiao, took place on the last day of the tournament. The winning team would advance to the North American Olympic Trials.

During the fifth game, my back became extremely painful, so painful that we had to call an injury timeout. The tumors on my spine tensed up so badly they were pinching a nerve. During the five-minute injury timeout, Sean used his paddle to loosen my back muscles, and I was able to resume play.

"When you're a coach, it's good to be able to wear a lot of hats," Sean later told a reporter. "These are things we had been preparing for all last week. We wanted to be ready for it."

Hugh and Xiao won the fifth game and took an early lead in the sixth. But we fought back to win the match four games to three, and advance to the North American Olympic Trials. Though we didn't advance to the U.S. Olympics, Sean and I had already qualified for the Paralympics in Athens.

"We just came here for some practice really, to get Tahl in a good, competitive situation before Athens," Sean told the reporter.

—Sean's Perspective—

As a former player who relished doubles, I proposed to Tahl that we enter the 2004 U.S. Olympic Doubles Trials. This unconventional playing partnership between coach and student would allow me to provide Tahl with valuable insights for confronting formidable opponents in high-pressure tournament situations. Tahl agreed, and we convened an intensive 11-day training camp in New York in preparation for the Washington D.C. trials where the top seven teams would vie for the coveted spot to represent the USA in the North American Olympic Doubles trials.

Doubles in table tennis is a symphony of balance that harmonizes each player's strengths while at the same time mitigating their individual weaknesses. We, however, were far from a balanced doubles team: a 28-year-old, 2465-rated Paralympic player with osteochondroma, and a 36-year-old, 2484-rated coach who hadn't seriously trained in eight years.

Tahl's driving force was a relentless pursuit of victory and a thirst for respect among his peers. For me, the joy of competition transcended wins and losses, thanks to my own mentor-coaches who specialized in periodization and used setbacks as fuel for feedback and improvement.

Periodization is the method of organizing training into separate blocks that focus on specific skills such as endurance, footwork, power, etc. In table tennis, the psychological game is so important that you can't expend your entire mental tank of energy each day in a do-or-die manner, so you must pace yourself.

Despite our differing goals — outcomes for Tahl, the thrill of competition for me — I knew our unique doubles partnership would be a distinct advantage at the Olympic trials. I also knew from my own experience having qualified for the 1988 and 1992 Olympics in singles, that the competition would be beneficial to Tahl's development as a table tennis competitor, irrespective of the result.

The competition at the 2004 U.S. Olympic Trials in Washington, D.C., was fierce. The top three teams would secure a berth in the North America Olympic Trials in Atlanta, just a few weeks away. Two formidable pairs, David Zhuang / Eric Owens and Mark Hazinski / Ilja Lupulesku, towered above the rest. That left the remaining five teams, including me and Tahl, battling for the third and final berth.

We triumphed over the weakest team with ease (4-1), suffered a tough loss to a left-handed duo (Reed and Cretu, 4-1), and then overcame the 2004 Olympic Singles qualifier Khoa Nguyen and his partner De Tran

(4-2), setting the stage for a thrilling tie-breaking finals match against the 2004 World Team Members Han Xiao and Adam Hugh, whose combined age of 33 years was exactly half of our total age.

Prior to the climactic final match, I offered Tahl some elementary pre-game advice: relax, step out, perhaps go for a brief run outside to clear his mind of self-induced stress. So what did he do? Called everybody in New York, including his wife, and told them he was one match away from qualifying for the North American Olympics trials, and then went on a two-mile sprint as if an invisible adversary was chasing him.

Moments before the match began, we were approached by the parents of our opponents. Adam Hugh's mother, Olympian Lily Yip, chimed in with a hint of caution. "This isn't going to be easy," she said. I responded resolutely, declaring our intent to treat this match as a final and drawing upon my wealth of experience in such high-pressure situations. Tahl mirrored my unwavering confidence. Little did I know he had depleted his energy with a sprint around the DC recreation center, leaving him on the brink of a full-body cramp.

We won the first game, conceded the second, rallied to take the third, and lost the fourth. At 9-9 in the fifth game, Tahl's body locked up, necessitating a brief injury timeout. Doing my best to massage out the full body cramp, I used everything at my disposal, including my paddle. Despite our efforts, we dropped the next point, trailing 3-2 in the best-of-seven match.

At this juncture, many teams might have considered defaulting. Not us. We redoubled our focus, choosing our shots judiciously, and came back from a 5-2 deficit to win the sixth game, 11-7. The best-of-seven game match was now tied, 3-3. Tahl and I were running on fumes, driven by sheer determination, like a plane out of fuel trying to land on a highway.

The seventh game held immeasurable weight. Each shot, each move, each decision resonated tenfold, with the audience perched on the edge of their seats. The young guns took an early lead, but the odd couple clawed back to tie the game at 6-6. A timeout called by Adam's father provided a moment of reflection. I reminded my partner, who was still remarkably stiff, that this wasn't just about table tennis; it was about grit and determination. Did we want it badly enough? Had we come this far only to let the opportunity slip away, or were we going to seize the victory?

Following the timeout, we snatched the next three points, inching ahead 6-9, and then momentarily stumbled, losing two quick points to bring the score to 8-9. Tahl then executed a perfect return, forcing an error, and we clinched the game, set and match.

The crowd erupted in a standing ovation as I hoisted the still-stiff Tahl in celebration. This match, this game seven, was profoundly significant for the future of our partnership. The trust and belief in each other we gained from this match paved the way for every future challenge to become a potential triumph, both on and off the table.

* * *

A Partner for Life

The bus ride back from Atlanta was sheer agony, but somehow I got home and went to bed. I was bedridden for the next two months, unable to stand or even go to the bathroom on my own. Dawn came over to my house every day and nursed me back to health.

Dawn's loving care sealed the deal. My search for a life-partner was over. The person I should marry was my best friend. The most important thing about a partnership, I now realized, is that both people in a relationship genuinely care about the well-being of their partner and try to make their lives better. Of course, there are other important aspects of a good marriage. But caring and helping are number one and two on my list of what defines a loving relationship, perhaps because I had little of that growing up.

A year after we met, in March of 2004, we were married in a church in Maspeth, Queens, where Dawn grew up.

Dawn and me in 2016

The 2004 Summer Paralympics in Athens

A few weeks after getting married, I traveled with Sean to Athens, Greece, to compete in the 2004 Summer Paralympics. Dawn, who doesn't enjoy traveling on a plane, stayed home. Here, again, is Sean's description of this tournament.

> *At the 2004 Summer Paralympics in Athens, Greece, the stage was set for me to help TEAM USA get to the winner's circle. All members were competitive and could taste Gold. For Tahl, he wanted to return to the winner's podium eight years after his triumphant performance at the 1996 Paralympics in Atlanta when he won a gold*

medal in the Class 7 Singles competition. Now he would be competing in the far more challenging Class 9 category.

Living in the Paralympic Village with Team USA, America's elite athletes, was an incredible experience. Tahl and I forged lifelong friendships with the volleyball coaches, cheered fervently for the women's Gold Medal-winning wheelchair basketball team, and lent our unwavering support to our quadriplegic wheelchair table tennis teammates.

In the table tennis team competition against Holland, Team USA came tantalizingly close to victory. After Tahl won his two singles matches in the team event, the gold medal depended on prevailing in the doubles match. Unfortunately, despite our valiant efforts, it wasn't meant to be. That's the nature of sports. Some days you triumph when the odds are stacked against you and your doubles' partner is battling full-body cramps. On other days, the ball simply takes an unexpected bounce and you lose the match.

Tahl faced a challenging path in the singles competition. In the first round, he fell to a Japanese player he had previously defeated in the U.S. Open, and was then pitted against one of the top seeds from Holland. After winning that hard-fought contest, he won his quarterfinal match against a player from Taipei who fell to Tahl's superior control and mastery. But in the semifinals, he lost to the top-seeded Austrian player who dropped just one game throughout the entire tournament.

Tahl still had one opportunity to win a medal. If he prevailed against the highly skilled Hungarian blocker in a best-of-five game match, he would win the bronze. This time, I made sure Tahl understood my advice to relax and step outside did not include multiple exciting telephone calls and a two-mile back-breaking sprint. My mantra was clear: one point at a time, and work relentlessly for each point.

Although Tahl started slowly in the first game, he won a resounding 3-0 victory. Team USA, thanks to Tahl's remarkable performance, secured a medal for our country's paralympic table tennis athletes. The awards ceremony with the Stars and Stripes proudly flying alongside the flags of Austria and China, was a resounding tribute to the indomitable spirit of Team USA and Tahl Leibovitz.

* * *

Mother's Deathbed Wish

Shortly after I returned from Athens, my mother boarded a train I was riding on and sat directly across from me. She didn't recognize me or pretended not to recognize me. Either was possible. I wasn't bothered. We hadn't said a word to each other since I took to the streets to avoid being beaten up by my father for breaking her basement window, a beating she thought I deserved. She blamed me for the problems in her life, and I thought she was a lousy parent. We had nothing to talk about.

A year later, when Maja told me our mother was battling Stage 4 breast cancer, I decided to put things right between us, work out our differences. When I visited her in hospital, she rambled on incoherently, obviously very stressed by her illness and impending death. But in a rare instance of lucidity, she encouraged me to go back to school and get a higher education.

"I always wanted more from you," she told me. "I want you to promise me one thing: That you will finish college."

I didn't want to tell her I had no intention of going to college. That I couldn't do basic math, so there was no way I could pass the college entrance exams.

But what she said stayed with me. Unlike my father, who demeaned all my efforts to succeed in life, my mother often encouraged me — the devil child whose birth saddled her with so much pain and misery — to get a higher education. Her deathbed admonishment to go back to school reflected the healthy side of her personality, the loving parent buried underneath all that craziness. I couldn't ignore her request.

* * *

Going back to school would have another benefit. It would help me wipe clean the stigma of flunking out twice at LaGuardia Community College, a failure that contradicted the core belief driving my development as a table tennis player: the self-confidence that if I did the hard work, practiced every day, mastered the nuances of spin and game strategy, I could become a top professional athlete in my chosen sport. Why should getting a college education be any different? Why couldn't

I apply that self-confidence and willingness to work hard into academic success?

* * *

When my mother was transferred into hospice, I decided to live with her during her final days in an effort to continue resolving the bad feelings between us. So I packed up my stuff and went to the hospice the next morning only to discover she had passed away during the night. She was 54.

Our long, troubled relationship was over. But at least it ended on a positive note. Without her deathbed encouragement, I might not have applied a few weeks later to the City University of New York's Adult Collegiate Program at Queens College — the only local university that would accept someone like me without a high school diploma and a 1.7 GPA.

My deficiency in mathematics once again let me down and I failed the entrance exam. But this time, I wasn't going to give up. Over the next five months, I studied up to 14 hours a day for the exam. Now that I had a roof over my head, was getting proper sleep, and no longer had to fight off people trying to steal my backpack, I could concentrate on my studies. When I retook the Queens College entrance exam, I passed it easily.

* * *

Table tennis makes you disciplined in many different areas. If you want to become a really good player, you have to practice for at least two hours every day. You have to compete. And if you want to win, you have to be super focused.

* * *

Later that year, Maja convinced me to run in the New York Marathon for Team Continuum, a cancer charity. Team Continuum was a client of Serious Celebrations, Maja's events management company. On mile seven of the marathon, I felt a sharp pain in the bottom of my right foot. Foot pain was not unusual for someone like me with deformed feet. Even today, I often experience foot pain during a table tennis match. But the pain I felt that day was really severe. After duct-taping the foot, I managed to walk slowly to the finish line. It took me 15 hours to complete the 26.2-mile marathon. People on crutches passed me along the way. I spent the next two weeks in bed, regretting that I hadn't trained for the marathon, though training might not have led to a different result.

I also wonder if today I'd finish the race. Probably yes, given my competitiveness and determination to never give up. It's difficult for a professional athlete to admit defeat, to stop fighting.

* * *

I always try to move towards the pain, accept it. People come into therapy thinking it will make everything bad go away, like anxiety and depression. But that seldom happens. It's much better to accept the pain and move on in life.

* * *

I did keep in contact with my dad. We talked on the phone occasionally. In 2005, a year before my mother died, I decided to meet him again in person. So I went to the pub in Queens where I knew he hung out. He was standing alone at the juke box, fumbling for coins to play a Roy Harper ballad. He still got drunk every night.

We sat down together at the bar. His face was very impassive. I started to speak in a very loud voice. I was very emotional.

"Dad, I want to tell you something," I said. "Do you remember when I was five years old and sick, you carried me from your bed into mine? I opened my eyes, but you didn't realize I was awake. So I closed my eyes and pretended I was still sleeping while you took me into my room and put me into my bed and laid my Curious George doll next to me."

"I wanted to tell you so bad that my eyes were open while you were carrying me. I wanted to tell you I was awake. For so long I have thought of this. I didn't think you remembered that day. I didn't think you cared if my eyes were open or not. And I wasn't sure it even mattered. So I never told you."

"I know, right now, you're looking into my eyes and still think I'm asleep, still don't see me. You probably won't even remember my visiting you today."

"But I have to tell you I'm not sleeping anymore. I'm so wide awake it burns my heart to even blink."

* * *

On one of my first days on the Queens College campus, I decided to introduce myself to Dr. Weitten, the school's athletic director. I walked into his office and put my backpack and a few other bags I was carrying on the floor. Before I could open my mouth, he said, in a very irritable tone of voice: "This isn't a garbage dump. This is an office!"

"Yes," I shot back, "but I want to tell you I'm a highly skilled table tennis player, and I want to represent the school in the collegiate championships."

That piqued his interest. He himself was a table tennis player, and Queens College had never won a collegiate championship in any sport. After I told him about my success in both able-bodied and Paralympic competitions, he arranged for the school to finance my participation in the competition.

Later that year, I won the gold medal in doubles and the silver medal in singles at the Collegiate National Championships. My toughest opponents were the non-English speaking Chinese and European players representing Texas Wesleyan University, a school known for its strong table tennis team.

Before enrolling at Queens College, I had applied to Texas Wesleyan for an athletic scholarship and was turned down because I competed in Paralympic tournaments and was therefore a person with physical disabilities. It didn't seem to matter to Texas Wesleyan that I was also one of the country's highest-rated able-bodied table tennis players and that I had won many medals at able-bodied tournaments.

At the Collegiate National Championships during the next four years, I beat all of the Texas Wesleyan competitors in 42 matches. That was incredibly satisfying!

The Athletic Director was the happiest man on our planet. For the first time in its history, Queens College was competitive in a college sport. He displayed my trophies in the school's gymnasium and helped me get financial aid to meet my educational expenses. It no longer mattered to him how many bags I dragged into his office. He no longer cared about that.

The world is full of well-meaning good people. Finding them is the problem.

* * *

My Demons Return

Once again, suicidal thoughts invaded my consciousness. I wondered if injecting air into my veins would finally eradicate those demons from my psyche — demons who didn't care about the positive things that were happening in my present life. So I consulted the school psychologist who pointed out that injecting air into my veins would be a very painful way to die. Hearing that was enough for me to abandon the idea.

The demons came back three years later. Dawn and I had been drifting apart for several months, and our marriage was on the verge of ending. She had formed a cover band for the Rolling Stones and I was still singing in a rock band — a mix between Tom Waits, Nirvana and the Yardbirds — that I had formed in 1999. When I was not performing, I was playing in table tennis tournaments in the U.S. and abroad. Dawn wanted me to give up my table tennis career so that we could spend more time together and not live so close to the bone, financially — a request that reengaged my persistent depression disorder and the terrible anxiety it caused. Table tennis was my anchor. Without it, I would be adrift in a sea of hurt.

This suicide attempt, I told myself, would be serious. Not like the half-hearted efforts of cutting my wrists lengthwise, avoiding the veins. Not like the fantasies of jumping in front of a subway car, or injecting air into my veins. This attempt would finally put my demons to rest.

So I bought two big bottles of spring water, parked my car at the Cross Street Bridge in Howard Beach, Queens, tied the bottles to my body and walked into the water. But it was winter, and the water was extremely cold. I just couldn't immerse myself in that icy grave.

Our relationship quickly recovered. We both gave up our singing careers, though Dawn's beautiful voice can still be heard when she sings in the choir of her church, the Living Word Ministry, which she joined in 2011 when she became a Born-Again Christian.

Dawns singing in her Church Choir

I came to Christ because I understood I was broken and needed help. I quit the cover band and stopped being angry all the time. I even started noticing people on the street who were homeless. When I told Tahl of my decision to become a Born-Again Christian, just like my mother had when she was also 36, Tahl said 'that was great.' He's very supportive.

-Dawn Leibovitz

Dawn spends a lot of time each day praying and reading, administering our private psychotherapy practice, and handing out food and clothing to people in need at her church. But being married to a professional athlete who's away for large chunks of time playing in tournaments halfway around the world is not easy. It's tough to be away on the road so much. We miss each other, worry about each other.

> *It's hard to live with a professional athlete who's on the road so much. It's hard to be alone for so long. I miss him, and worry about him. Sometimes, I travel with him to local tournaments. But I don't like to fly, and, believe it or not, I really like to be home.*
>
> *-Dawn Leibovitz*

* * *

Having finally hurdled over the college entrance exam, my academic career really took off. In 2010, I graduated from Queens College with a 3.2 GPA and bachelor's degrees in Sociology and Philosophy. My interest in these subjects was stimulated by two books I read, The Power Elite by C. Wright Mills, and Plato's The Dialogues.

Earning BA's in Philosophy and Sociology was more satisfying than winning any table tennis championship or medal. Graduating from college is very difficult, especially for someone like me who skipped a grade school education.

* * *

President Obama and me during the White House visit
of the U.S. Paralympic Team after returning from
the Rio Paralympic Games in 2016

In 2011, I earned an MUA (Master of Urban Affairs) at Queens College with a 3.9 GPA, and then matriculated to the graduate school at Touro College in Forest Hills. Touro was a lot cheaper than most other institutions of higher learning, and I wanted to save money. But the school was very disorganized and fights broke out among the students just about every day. When I complained to Dawn about Touro, she said: "Why don't you just transfer to another school?"

A table tennis student of mine at the time, Dov Kolker, an Israeli-born orthopedist on the staff of Mt. Sinai in New York City, encouraged me to apply to NYU's Silver School of Social

117

Work. Dov has always had a positive influence on my life as both a friend and mentor. In return, I've helped him transition from a top 300 world ranked tennis player to a much better-than-average table tennis competitor.

* * *

Dr. Dov spends an inordinate amount of his free time doing pro bono work helping people with medical, physical and other disabilities. Fueled by a bottomless empathy for the disadvantaged, he sets a very high bar for me to reach.

* * *

Encouraged by both Dawn and Dov, I did apply to New York University's Silver School of Social Work a few weeks later, and was accepted. NYU had a great table tennis team with Michael Landers and other talented players, and it's one of the best schools in the country for studying clinical social work. Michael and I did compete for NYU at the 2014 Collegiate National Championships.

Michael Landers (left) and me (right) with Eric Boggan,
the greatest U.S. table tennis player of all time.

Finding time for table tennis practice was difficult. Before enrolling at LaGuardia College in 2006, I practiced at least 35-40 hours a week. Once back in school, practice time was reduced to 6-10 hours a week. At NYU, where I was enrolled in 16 class credits and required to put in 30 hours of clinical work each week to qualify for the state licensing exam, practice time was rare. Some weeks, I could not play at all because of midterms and final exams.

In 2015, I graduated from NYU with a master's degree in social work (M.S.W.) with a GPA of 3.8.

Originally, I thought I would become a psychologist, but I had trouble mastering statistics. Then I learned about social work and found it much more interesting than psychology. Generally speaking, psychologists focus on the individual's problems; social workers focus on those factors that contribute to an individual's problems — family life, institutions. social systems, the environment, etc. The latter approach was far more appealing to me and made more sense to me, given my backstory.

* * *

At the London Paralympics in 2012, I noticed that the umpire for my first match was impeccably dressed and meticulous in both speech and movement. Every article of clothing, from his bow tie to his socks, had obviously been carefully chosen. And though he walked with a crutch and struggled to move even a few feet, every step he took was orchestrated. It seemed to me he was desperately trying to fool the world into believing he was a normal able-bodied person. And that really bothered me.

"Just live your life," I wanted to tell him. "You're handicapped. It sucks, but accept it."

Watching him struggle to put pens into his shirt pocket, a simple task that was taking him several minutes to accomplish, the urge to speak finally overwhelmed me.

"Look, you're a very particular person," I told him. "You are disabled, and you cannot control your disability by controlling the external world."

I was pretty sure I knew what I was talking about. This umpire was trying to control external aspects of the world because his disability was uncontrollable. He looked confused by my outburst, perhaps because his mastery of the English language was not very good.

In retrospect, I now realize I was talking to my former self, to that person who for so many years masqueraded as a normal, able-bodied person. And though what I said about not being able to control the external world might make sense, I had no right to be so impatient with him. My physical disabilities were nowhere near as debilitating or obvious as his were. It was a lot easier for me to hide my physical handicaps, which I did until I joined the U.S. Paralympic team.

Angie and Stellan

In 2013, I came under the wings of two other remarkable Paralympic coaches, Stellan Bengtsson, the great Swedish player, and his Native American wife, Angie. Stellan won three world, seven European and 65 international championships. Angie is a ten-time U.S. National Champion and a member of the United States Association of Table Tennis' Hall of Fame.

Stellan taught me how to make the game very simple. "Many players over-complicate the game," he told me. "A good player breaks the game down to its simplest elements." He also stressed the need to keep moving both feet throughout a match. Many coaches overcomplicate their teaching. Stellan keeps it simple and smart.

In 1971, Stellan was the world's top ranked player.

Angie was my match coach. We spent a lot of time together, traveling to and playing at tournaments. In 2015, we won the Pan Am Games. The following year we got to the quarter finals of the Paralympic Games where I lost to the eventual gold medal winner.

Angie was always very positive and relaxed, and could calm me down when I got overheated or upset during a match. Which still happens, though not as often as it once did.

Angie coaching me during a match

I remember having dinner with Angie one night at a tournament. We were discussing team unity when suddenly she went quiet. "My sister-in-law has cancer," she said." When I get back home, I will be with her helping her get through chemotherapy."

Angie's remark left me speechless. I thought about how tough it was watching my mother unsuccessfully battle cancer. Team unity, the tournament itself, even table tennis, seemed really insignificant compared to a family member battling cancer.

For so many years, table tennis had been my one safe harbor where I could escape from real-world problems. But now, finally, I was doing more than just surviving off-the-court and relying on table tennis as my special therapy. I was confronting real-life head-on. My mother's illness and death, falling in love with and marrying Dawn, and the positive influence and wisdom of my coach-mentors — Sean, Dov, Stellan and Angie — helped me put table tennis in its proper perspective, and thereby achieve a healthy balance between my professional and personal life.

* * *

To be a successful professional athlete, you have to isolate real-world distractions while training and competing. But to be a healthy human being off the court, you have to let those problems in and deal with them as best you can.

* * *

At the Paralympic Pan American Games in Vancouver (2015) and Lima (2019), I was pitted against formidable Mexican adversaries in the finals of the Class 9 competitions. In Lima, my coach called a timeout with my opponent up 7-3 in the final and deciding game. The outlook was rather grim. I remembered Sean's words when years earlier I was faced with a similarly desperate match challenge.

"No one really cares about your results other than your wife, Dawn, and myself," he told me. "The Chinese, the Swedes, don't dwell on them, and the U.S. Olympic Committee (USOC) focuses on overall team success. The onus of caring falls on you.

"At the end of the day, you're blessed with an incredible life, a wonderful wife, and you're out there playing for the sheer joy of competition. You thrive as a warrior in the arena, pitting your skills against like-minded rivals."

Drawing strength from these words, the burden of pressure and tension gripping me during the match fell away, and I strung together six consecutive points to go up 9-7. Only two points away from a victory that would clinch a spot at the 2020 Paralympics in Tokyo, I lost the next three critical points and now faced a match point.

Another piece of Sean's shared wisdom, something he himself learned from Werner Schlager of Austria, the former World Champion, came to mind. Schlager had achieved remarkable victories over two Chinese players after facing match points in both matches.

"When an opponent faces no pressure, holding a match point," Sean told me, "They become most susceptible to an upset."

Remembering those words of wisdom revived my confidence, and I won the next three points to win the game, 12-10, and a place at the 2020 Paralympic Games.

When I won the Class 9 singles final at the 2019 Paralympic
Pan American in Lima, my Mexican opponent collapsed in tears.
I picked him up and tried to console him.

Me and my coach, Mitchell Seidenfeld, the great
American Paralympic champion, at the 2019
Parapan American Games in Lima

Such is the beauty of table tennis, a sport of lightning-quick momentum shifts where fortunes can reverse in the blink of an eye. Tahl summoned his inner strength and skill to win the match. His triumph encapsulated the age-old adage — the thrill of victory and the agony of defeat —underscoring the profound emotions and relentless determination that drive athletes like him to play, compete, and, triumph.

-Sean O'Neill

U.S. Hall of Fame Induction

December 17, 2015. The Flamingo Hotel. Las Vegas. My coach, friend and mentor, Sean O'Neill, is introducing me as a newly inducted member of the United States Association of Table Tennis' Hall of Fame. The dining room is crowded with past and present players, including Jim Butler and George Braithwaite, two of table tennis' all-time greats.

"One day, Tahl and his buddies found a new activity at the Boys and Girls Club in Queens," says Sean. "It wasn't world-class table tennis but wood and sandpaper paddles, a beat-up sawhorse table and a wobbly ball. The perfect game for the short in stature, but big-in-heart New Yorker."

Two of my childhood friends, Glenn Brown and Santo Vasquez, who also discovered table tennis at that youth club 25 years ago, are here at my Hall of Fame induction ceremony. Both are highly accomplished medal-winning competitors.

"In conclusion," Sean adds, "it sometimes comes up in interviews that Tahl was homeless for many years as a kid. Well, I think it is obvious that Tahl has always had a home in table tennis and I would like to introduce this years' newest USATT Hall of Fame inductee, Tahl Leibovitz."

I am filled with mixed feelings, all good. Proud to be recognized as a table tennis champion who has won medals in both Paralympic and able-bodied tournaments. But not yet ready to give up the competitive spirit that still burns inside me.

* * *

127

A year later, in the quarterfinals at the 2016 Paralympic Games in Brazil, I played the No.1 player from Belgium. Winning would have placed me in the medal round. The first and third games were very close. I had a lot of trouble with his short forehand serve and he eventually won the match. For the first time in my plus 20 years of competition, I felt comfortable with the loss. Finally, there were enough good, positive things going on in my life that I understood winning or losing doesn't define who I really am. This newfound perspective helped me win many more championships in the upcoming years.

Social Work

During my first year of study at NYU's School of Social Work, I was required to serve a student internship at the East New York Clubhouse in Brooklyn, a community-based psychiatric rehabilitation center. On my first day at the facility, I walked into the lounge area where a middle-aged man was playing the piano.

"I enjoy listening to you play the piano," I said.

"I play piano. I sing. I write poetry," the man replied. "You have to do something to pass the time here."

The man spoke slowly, as if he was heavily medicated. Neither of us felt like continuing the conversation, so I walked over to a nearby bookcase and picked out a book — a very heavy Advanced Biology textbook.

"Is this your first day?" a middle-aged woman standing behind me asked. I turned around.

"Yeah," I replied. "I guess so."

I wasn't looking to have an extended dialogue with any of the residents on this my first day as an intern. I just wanted to observe, maybe watch some TV, ease myself gently into this new and unusual environment without drawing any attention to myself.

The woman was wearing a Spring dress and spoke English with a German accent. She was an attractive silver-haired woman of about 60. She had dark red nail polish on her left hand, and dark black polish on her right hand. She pointed to the textbook I was holding.

"Advanced biology is not really advanced," she said. "It's just more material to memorize after you finish with basic biology. Same thing with chemistry and microbiology. That's what you do to get your bachelor's degree. Memorize and regurgitate and throw it all up on your professor's lap because you really don't know what you're talking about."

"Okay," I said. "What about a master's degree? What do you do to get one of those?"

"A master's degree is different," she replied. "You have to create original content. You're no longer vomiting on your professor. You're giving the professor bottles of wine, flowers and fruit."

I noticed two Dominican individuals sitting next to each other on the couch: a woman in her mid-twenties, and a rather small teenager who was talking rapidly in Spanish. The woman was staring at the ceiling in silence. To my left, an African American man was pacing back and forth, talking to himself.

"Aren't you going to respond to me," the woman asked. She was obviously agitated.

"I don't know what to say," I said.

"Are you a member here?" the piano player asked.

"I am not a member here," I replied. "I am your new social worker."

Over the next few weeks, I got to know the people who lived in the clubhouse. The piano player had stabbed his mother 45 times due to a drug-induced psychosis. We ended up becoming friends, and a few years later, he moved into his own apartment.

The German woman's four-year-old daughter was killed by a drunk driver while playing in her front yard in Germany, and her eight-year-old son was killed a week later in a car crash. She was driving.

Another clubhouse member told me her three brothers were murdered in front of her by her mother in a snowstorm.

My life was a lot easier than many of the people here.

During my nine-month internship, I ran a DTR (Double Trouble Recovery) 12 step program for clubhouse members struggling with drug addiction and mental illness. I also ran a Wednesday afternoon computer class, engaged members in social activities — bingo, board games and table tennis — and helped them prepare for transition to life and employment outside the clubhouse.

This experience was an amazing beginning to my career as a social worker. The East New York Clubhouse is a remarkable community where over 400 members build positive relationships with staff that promote self-esteem and self-confidence — the bedrock of healthy change.

It is also a community that embodies one of the core principles of the Social Work Code of Ethics, that dignity and personal worthiness play a vital part in the relationship between social workers and the people they serve.

People struggling with mental illness are often told how to feel and behave. This approach is polarizing. A much more effective approach is a partnership between the social worker and the people they serve — a partnership of mutual respect.

The collective approach by the members and staff of the East New York Clubhouse taught me more about myself than I could learn on my own.

* * *

I also interned for the HOPE program, an organization providing training, education, job placement and lifelong support to young adults in need of help. One of my jobs was to take part in the organization's Homeless Outreach Population Estimate's Annual Survey of Homelessness. I was assigned to Penn Station where I randomly stopped people and asked them if they had a place to live. Of the first 100 people I stopped, 60 said they had no home to go to.

Homelessness is invisible to most people. People don't generally see homeless people unless they live or work in the prominent areas where panhandling is common and the symbiotic relationship between homeless people and people with money thrives.

* * *

The next important chapter in my life — finding work that was more than just a means of financing my table tennis career — was starting. Work that was meaningful for other people, not just for me.

* * *

In 2015, after receiving a Master of Social Work degree from NYU's Silver School of Social Work, my next step was to take the Master of Social Work State Exam.

Graduation Day; NYU Silver School of Social Work

Passing the exam was a prerequisite for obtaining a license to practice social work. As a recent grad, the knowledge needed to pass the exam was still very fresh in my mind. But over the next six months, I scheduled and then rescheduled the exam repeatedly.

133

Sean realized there was a problem. "I'm not ready to take the LMSW test," I told him. "I need more time to prepare."

"Take the test," he advised. "Even if you fail, you can turn that failure into a positive experience. "You'll have a better understanding of the test, and the next time you take it, you'll pass."

A few weeks later, I took the test and passed with a very high score.

* * *

One of my psychotherapy clients wanted to change his life. He was 31 years old and had lived most of his life in foster homes because his mother was addicted to crack. After failing the psychological section of the police exam, the last obstacle to becoming a police officer, he decided he wanted to become a therapist. Not the easiest goal.

He came under my care after checking himself into a psychiatric hospital because he believed he was "mentally unstable." In fact, he had not slept for almost four days, something that could make anyone feel mentally unsound.

A year later, after he was accepted into a Master of Social Work Program, we sat in my office talking. He was worried he would fail in graduate school.

"If you forget everything about our work together, it's totally okay," I told him. "But if you remember one thing, remember this: it's easy to accomplish something when there are no obstacles."

"I know that because you and I have had similar paths," he replied.

* * *

In 2017, I was invited to speak at the United Nations along with other recipients of the Moroccan government's Champion of Sport and Peace award. What follows is an edited version of what I said:

First of all, it's great to be here. We've had some very good speakers today. I won't be too long.

One of the earlier speakers talked about marginalized people, the people I try to help as a social worker. In this world, to create division between people, we have to create a story about them being inadequate or deficient and just not as good as we are. We diminish their humanity so that we can hurt and harm them.

One of the things I like about sport is that diminishing someone else's humanity rarely occurs. Sport is a shared endeavor. If we compete as part of a team, we have unity. And without opponents, we could not compete or achieve success. So all of us, teammates and opponents, have a shared passion for the sport and a shared humanity.

There is a table tennis player in the audience. His name is Ahmed and he is from Egypt. I was born in Israel. Ahmad and I are completely different. Our cultures are different. But we are good friends. He is helping me as my coach, helping me to become a better table tennis player. When we speak with each other,

135

our different opinions on many important matters are obvious. But when we practice table tennis, we have a connection that makes those differences of opinion invisible and unimportant.

Table Tennis was very helpful for me. I was unschooled and homeless as a boy for most of my teenage years. But every day, for four hours, I practiced table tennis at a boy's club until I became very good at the sport. And that success gave me the confidence to go back to school, earn two master's degrees and eventually become a social worker.

I was also fortunate to have a coach and mentor, Sean O'Neill, a former table tennis champion. Without Sean, I definitely would not be here today.

* * *

I was sitting alone in the Paralympic Village at the end of the 2020 Summer Paralympics in Tokyo after all my friends and fellow competitors had gone home, when I was overcome with an emptiness I hadn't felt for years. An emptiness that consumed me throughout my childhood and many years of teenage homelessness. I was not depressed. I was depression itself.

So I opened an internal dialogue between the 47-year-old practicing psychotherapist I had become and the depressed, suicidal teenager of my past. And then, slowly, I realized what I was experiencing was disconnection from others, something I often feel. This feeling, I told myself, cannot last forever. I would be leaving Japan the next day, returning to my usual environment of authentic connections and meaningful activities, and the emptiness would go away.

Which it did.

On a five-mile hike during the 2024
Slovenia Paralympics Open

The Present

Today, I work with children, adults and veterans struggling to cope with a wide array of mental and physical disabilities from autism and bipolar disorder to schizophrenia and substance abuse. I also run eight-to-ten group therapy sessions a week for the New York Dept. of Mental Health and Hygiene, and maintain a private practice in Sea Cliff, Long Island.

I also do a lot of volunteer work, helping people get through school, improve their lives, and alleviate their suffering. In this way, I am recognizing all the great mentoring I've received and trying to give back.

Like Plato said, we should be kind to other people.

When you add my worktime to the time I devote to table tennis — practicing and playing in tournaments in the U.S. and abroad — there really isn't much time left for anything else in my life.

In 2016, I founded a national company called Project Table Tennis, a community-based program of activities and events that utilize table tennis as a vehicle to create meaningful relationships between people. Project Table Tennis sponsors team-based activities involving adults, children and seniors struggling with Alzheimer's, autism, obesity, physical disabilities and substance abuse. It embodies my core belief that sport is a powerful unifier, something we do together as spectators, coaches and competitors. It is a collective endeavor. It is both personal and environmental.

Sean serves as the CIO of Project Table Tennis. He maintains our website, updates my iPad and home security systems, and reminds me when to file our company's quarterly taxes on time!

In the mental health field, many specialists differentiate between the "individual" and the "collective" when they search for solutions to mental disorders. Some specialists believe solutions can be found in analyzing how a person relates to him or herself; other specialists believe solutions can be found in an understanding of how individuals relate to their environment. I believe solutions can be found in both the person and the environment.

Today, I am seriously training for the 2024 Paralympic Games which will be held in Paris in August. Training includes walking 20,000 steps every day, practicing table tennis at least 40 hours a week, and restricting my diet to healthy foods of no more than 1600 calories a day.

My typical daily diet is:

Breakfast — Greek yogurt with walnuts, blueberries and a tablespoon of honey.

Lunch — Tuna salad and a wrap with spinach, eggs and cheese.

Mid-Afternoon —Macha tea without sugar.

Dinner — Grilled chicken salad.

It is more than enough to sustain my high energy lifestyle!

Afterthoughts

One of the practitioners of European Existential Psychotherapy, Emmy Van Durezen, says there are four dimensions to human existence: physical, personal, social and spiritual.

Physical existence is defined by the fragility of human existence and the anxiety of knowing we can die at any moment.

Personal existence is our struggle to understand how we want to live our lives and who we want to be.

The social dimension is defined by how we relate to others.

The spiritual dimension asks the question of how we want to live.

In my work as a psychotherapist, many of my patients have a strong problem in one or more of those areas. They are difficult with themselves or with others. If I can help them accept themselves and other people, the world becomes a much more manageable place.

When I was homeless, I had difficulty with all four dimensions of human existence. Why was I rejected by my parents? Why are others on the street constantly trying to harm me? Why is the world so remote, cold and violent? Who was I becoming, and who did I want to become?

Those were the questions I desperately wanted to answer.

Eventually, I realized that these questions cannot always be answered, that life is at times both unpredictable and uncontrollable. So you have to adapt.

It's much the same in a table tennis match. Your opponent will do something you haven't anticipated, and if you don't adapt your tactics, your game, you will lose.

For Serious Table Tennis Players

The problem today for many players is they focus on becoming a top player at the very beginning of their careers. They do not experience the competetive steppingstones that over time honed my skills and competitiveness. At the South Queens Boy's Club, my motivation was to beat the other players who were much better than me. At the Lost Battalion Club, I had to once again raise my level of play to win games against players who were also much better than me. And, finally, after becoming a tournament player, I had to again raise my skill level to compete successfully against professional players from all over the world.

The truly great thing about table tennis is you can improve your game at any age. I coach people in their 80s who work hard at improving their play with great success. Compared to other people who do not exercise regularly, they are in good physical shape. Unlike recreational players, they move their feet quickly and constantly during a match.

But to play the game at my professional level, you have to be in excellent physical condition, and the older you are, the harder you must work at maintaining your conditioning.

Having the proper mental attitude is also crucial. Sean O'Neill, my longtime coach and mentor, taught me never to worry about the results of a match or worry about satisfying others. No other coach I've had pays more attention to the psychological aspect of the sport than Sean.

143

Sean also introduced me to video analysis. Watching recordings of myself and my opponents has helped me identify my playing weaknesses and strengths. Intermediate-level players can also benefit from watching videos of them playing. Game tactics and strategy depend on an understanding of an opponent's strengths and weaknesses.

Table Tennis is a game of deception. We try to get our opponents to commit to a certain style of playing, and then we deceive them. We add more spin than they anticipate, smash the ball when they expect a topspin return, and hit a no spin dead ball when they expect a spiny loop.

Sometimes, when we deceive our opponents, we also deceive ourselves, unconsciously. We become overly critical or overly confident of our performance. We imagine how the game should be played and what the results should be. We lose our ability to adapt to the unexpected twists and turns of a match. We try to deceive our opponent, and, instead, deceive ourselves.

Successful match play is a product of practice and training that replicates competition and builds confidence. Practice is the best antidote to both false confidence and a lack of confidence.

When I play a match, I try to inhabit a Zenlike state, similar to sleep, where I allow the game to come to me. Whatever tactics my opponent employs does not surprise or disturb me. I adapt and let my dependable technique effectively counter.

Of course, being human, I am not always successful. Sometimes I relapse into self-critical anger. But more often I do not. Adaptability is the key. On the table tennis court, and in real life.

Match Results

—Paralympic Games—

Atlanta 1996
–Men's Singles C7 (Gold)
–Men's Teams C6-8 (Bronze)

Taipei 2002
–Quarterfinals

Athens 2004
–Men's Singles C9 (Bronze)

Atlanta 2008
–Undefeated in Team Event

—Parapan American Games—

Rio de Janeiro 2007
–Men's Singles C8 (Gold)
–Open Singles Standing (Gold)
–Men's Teams C8 (Gold)

Guadalajara 2011
–Men's Singles C9 (Gold)
–Men's Teams C9-10 (Silver)

Toronto 2015
–Men's Singles C9 (Gold)
–Men's Teams C9-10 (Silver)

Lima 2019
–Men's Singles C9 (Gold)
–Men's Teams C9-10 (Bronze)

Santiago 2023
–Men's Singles C9 (Gold)
–Men's Doubles C8-10 (Bronze)

—Paralympic World Championships—

Paris 1998
–Men's Teams C10 (Bronze)

—Able-Bodied Tournaments—

Queens, New York State Championships 1998
–Men's Open Singles (Gold)

Collegiate Championships 2008
–Men's Singles (Silver)
–Men's Doubles (Gold)
–Mixed Doubles (Silver)

Collegiate Championships 2009
–Men's Doubles (Gold)

—Maccabiah Games—

1997
–Able-Bodied Team (Bronze)
–Able-Bodied Mixed Doubles (Bronze)

2013
–Para Open Singles (Gold)

2021
–Para Open Singles (Gold)
–Able-Bodied Men's Doubles (Bronze)

Sean's Afterword

During this summer of 2023, I found myself facing an unfamiliar and daunting situation as a father. My daughter, Kaitlyn, was on a journey to explore her passion for attending a musical theatre college, immersing herself in Broadway shows, and participating in a two-week summer pre-college camp at the prestigious American Musical and Dance Academy (AMDA). As a father out of his element, I turned to Tahl for assistance and guidance.

Tahl, ever the kind-hearted and generous soul, dropped everything he was doing and devoted his time and energy to ensure that Kaitlyn's three-week super-intensive New York City experience would be nothing short of exceptional. He made certain we had transportation, food, and all the guidance necessary to navigate this exciting adventure. Tahl's efforts extended to everyday tasks like shopping for bed sheets at TJ Maxx, finding summer reading material at libraries, and even late-night pickups in the city to spare us from taking the late-night Long Island Railroad (LIRR) back to his home.

Airport pick-ups, delightful Boba Tea stops, and leisurely walks around Sea Cliff to log our daily steps were all part of the meticulously planned itinerary. Tahl treated my daughter as if she were a member of his own family, ensuring she had everything she needed for her camp and audition. His support was unwavering and selfless, regardless of the inconvenience it may have caused him.

Ever competitive and not one to be outdone, I reciprocated the kindness. I collaborated with Tahl's twin sister, Maja, at the club, offering valuable insights to help enhance her forehand and backhand techniques, ultimately contributing to her enjoyment of league play at the Gold Coast TTC. It was a true pleasure to assist Maja in her pursuit of improvement, a reminder that I, too, share Tahl's competitive spirit, albeit in the realm of doing good deeds.

In a heartwarming twist of fate, we received incredible news at the end of the summer: Kaitlyn was accepted into AMDA, a testament to her talent and hard work.